To Josh

What I learned
in the wild is
yours for the
taking

Best

Bobby C

PRAISE FOR
MASTERS OF THEIR UNIVERSE

"Practical and valuable lessons are brought to life through vividly described anecdotes written in a heartfelt tone with a subtle (yet evident) sense of humor. This book was a joy to read. The practical wisdom that's applied to very complex situations will engage readers. Secret after secret, page after page, one is inspired to reflect on one's own behavior and the challenges we face in business and in private life. Wisdom blends so seamlessly with a captivating story."

—Oris R. Stuart III
CEO and Managing Partner, Global Novations,
A Korn/Ferry International Company

"A highly readable, fascinating book from Bobby Haas, himself a two-legged Master of the Universe. Sure to become a favorite at schools of business everywhere."

—Roger Enrico
Retired Chairman and CEO, PepsiCo
Former Executive Chairman, DreamWorks Animation SKG

"'Genius' is my least favorite word in the English language, and I resist its use at all costs. But Masters of Their Universe forces me to break my rule. Bobby Haas can claim that unique status in two very separate worlds—business and art. Blending those disparate realms together in Masters is awe-inspiring."

—James H. Berick
Retired Partner, Squire Sanders

"Masters of Their Universe has brilliantly woven tales from the boardroom and the bush into an insightful reflection on the true nature of success. This book demonstrates both acute observational acumen and intuitive sensitivity to the wisdom of our four-legged brethren. A captivating new perspective on the phrase 'survival of the fittest.'"

—Michael Cappello, MD
Director, Yale University World Fellows Program

MASTERS OF THEIR UNIVERSE

Business (and Life) Secrets Taught by
Four-Legged Professors

MASTERS OF THEIR UNIVERSE

Business (and Life) Secrets Taught by Four-Legged Professors

Robert B. Haas

Langdon Street Press

Langdon Street Press
212 3rd Avenue North, Suite 290
Minneapolis, MN 55401
612.455.2293
www.langdonstreetpress.com

ISBN-13: 978-1-62652-229-9
LCCN: 2013942948

Distributed by Itasca Books

Book design by Kristeen Ott

Printed in the United States of America

Any book devoted to the wisdom imparted by four-legged creatures should be dedicated solely to four-legged creatures. And so it is with this book, which is dedicated to the parade of canines in our family who have shared our home over the years. To the members of Oliver's illustrious clan, both those who are still warm and fuzzy and the ones who are warm no more: Oliver, Elmer, Chloe, Henry, Spencer, and Cooper. And to our latest rescues in the post-Oliver era, Murphy and Baxter, who have never seen their names in print, until now.

Acknowledgments

Too often, the words *brilliant* and *friend* litter the contents of an Acknowledgments page as well as our everyday speech. In certain English-speaking cultures, *brilliant* is casually applied to almost any idea that has been cooked beyond the state of being half-baked, and no adjective is left to describe the few truly radiant thoughts that have not lost their luster through overuse of that label. And the designation *friend* has become a rather mushy term that seems to have no edges to define its borders. I once commented that in the banter at black-tie affairs, the social networks of the attendees could often be divided into only two compartments: someone that the conversationalist had never met before and self-proclaimed "close personal friends."

But the word *partner* is one that has resisted the corrosive effects of time and social convention and emerged relatively unscathed, with its original intent largely intact. And for that reason, I wish to acknowledge the *partners* who have played a crucial role in my life's work as related in this book: to Candice, my marital partner of forty-four years and fellow traveler along a journey that has produced our daughters Samantha, Courtney, and Vanessa, son Gavin, and granddaughter Milly; to the long list of business partners (both those who toiled within the four walls of our investment firms and the ones who managed our portfolio companies), whose exploits can never be separated from what may generously be attributed to me; and to my editor Rebecca Ascher-Walsh, who was truly my partner in developing the manuscript for this book.

Author's Note

Throughout the book, I use quotes when recounting conversations for dramatic effect. The text in quotes should not be attributed as the actual words or opinions of the speaker, but rather to reflect my impression and best recollection of the approximate content of the conversation.

Contents

Preface

I AM A FIRM BELIEVER THAT LIFE SHOULD be lived in the headlong pursuit of passion. I have long felt that if I wake up in the morning and do not steer my body and mind in the direction of an enterprise fueled by gusto, then that is a day that is wasted. It is squandering a measure of time when I have no earthly idea how much more time is mine to squander.

My adult life has been consumed in the pursuit of one passion after another—often fitfully and sometimes erratically, but always chasing some distant horizon. The world of high finance captured my fascination and monopolized my time after I left the practice of law at the age of thirty-one in favor of the burgeoning field of venture capital. With no formal training in finance, I forfeited the security of a law partnership and positioned myself squarely at the bottom of a totem pole in a boutique investment firm. Driven more by ambition than sense, I set my sights on reaching the distant horizon of long-term financial security.

Though my brief venture capital career was eminently forgettable, the lessons gained lasted long after the bruises to my self-esteem had faded. Convinced that there was a better path to my version of the Promised Land, I moved to the newly emerging world of leveraged buyouts (LBOs), where the potential rewards for "first movers" in the field—the buyout shops that ventured into this frontier before it was overrun with competitors—were colossal indeed. The senior partners in a 1980s-vintage LBO firm could fulfill the ambitions of a lifetime before the decade had run its course. And a few of us so-called masters of the universe did just that. Between 1984 and 1989, our buyout firm racked up a series of tape-measure home runs. After a short-lived blitzkrieg of deals, that distant horizon of financial security was distant no more.

Once the warm fuzzy blanket of security was firmly within my grasp, I felt gratified and disoriented at the same time. I was thrilled to have placated the ambitions that gnawed at my gut, but also at a complete loss as to what to do next. So I did the only logical thing there was to do—on the spur of the moment, I went out and bought some camera gear at the age of forty-seven and headed for the wilds of Kenya.

I had no idea what I was searching for in Kenya, but it didn't seem to matter. I just needed a bit of time away from old familiar haunts. For reasons that may forever remain as mystical as the continent itself, I immediately felt at home in Africa. I felt as if I belonged there. The wilderness was everything the world of finance was not. Except for the occasional safari guide, there was rarely anyone else around—it was peaceful, it was natural, it was primeval. And it was populated with animals that went about their business consumed only by hunger and thirst and not greed or jealousy. It was a journey back in time and away from the invasion of modernity and its gadgets into my life. It was a place where a simple point-and-shoot camera replaced a phalanx of computers and cell phones. It was a way to lose myself and find my bearings among creatures that knew nothing of my other world, sometimes having never seen a two-legged being or a four-wheeled vehicle before. In a word, it was spellbinding.

Preface

Africa was my proving ground as a photographer. In that once-dark continent, I embarked on a new career that would eventually lead to the hallowed halls of National Geographic and the improbable launch of a series of photographic books with my name and the famed yellow rectangle of the Geographic on their covers.

From the outset, I was captivated by the life-and-death drama that unfolds in the theater of the African wilderness. One phenomenon after another is more wondrous than the ones witnessed the day before—elephant herds that are matriarchal in their governance despite the superior heft of adult bulls, an exquisitely maned lion holding sway over an entire pride of lionesses and their offspring, an elegant cheetah strutting around in blissful bachelordom after impregnating a female who would be left on her own to raise vulnerable cubs.

The social fabric that knits together a clan in the wild was never more fascinating to me than the one at work within the rare packs of African wild dogs (also known as painted wolves) that I photographed in Botswana. Faintly resembling German shepherds, wild dogs appear to have been assembled at a dysfunctional factory where ears that are too large are attached to a chassis that is too narrow and finished with a paint job that is too abstract. But what this mammal lacks in classic beauty it more than makes up for in hunting prowess and devotion to its clan.

The hardier members of the wild dog pack will at times take great pains to care for their injured brethren by returning from a kill with morsels in their bellies and then regurgitating fresh meat for the less able. Hunted to near extinction by man, the wild dog survives to this day on its stamina, its cunning, and its devotion to the sanctity of the clan. Every member of the pack has become a critical link to the destiny of the species.

I had my own pack of "wild" dogs back home in Dallas. Not exactly painted wolves that would disembowel their prey before larger predators pounced on the carcass, but an odd assortment of mixed breeds that welcomed my return from more primitive climes and captured my attention much like the creatures half a globe away. Once I arrived home after each photo shoot and tossed the weathered contents of my duffel bags into the laundry, I found solace in the company of my clan of mutts whose ancestral roots trace back to the gray wolves of more feral days.

After years of pressing the viewfinder of the camera against my eye, a strange phenomenon began to take hold even after those cameras had been stored away on the shelf awaiting my next trip into the wilderness—I continued to feel as if the camera were still an appendage to my arm and my eyes were searching for something worthy of capture. I was focused more intensely on the world around me.

The time spent with my pack of half-breeds was certainly no exception. I began to detect in their behavior faint vestiges of their wolf heritage. Although separated by thousands of years from the prehistoric wilds of the North American plains, the gang of mutts that roamed my backyard exhibited some of the fundamentals of clan dynamics passed down from distant ancestors. I was surprised at how many of their instinctive habits no longer served any survival function at all but simply endured from one generation to the next: kicking back dirt to cover fresh droppings, rolling in another animal's feces (imitating the ruse of their forebears to mask their scent when sneaking up on prey), the playful tug-of-war at opposite ends of a bone (used by young predators to sharpen their fighting skills), and spray-marking the choice locations on our property to declare territorial rights.

At first, I thought of the clan's array of vestigial habits as rather quaint—an amusing but anachronistic echo of the days when wolves lorded over vast swaths of the American landscape. But the habits also revealed something more intriguing and enlightening. The creatures in the raw savannah and the ones in my own backyard were both dancing the practiced steps of a minuet known as *survival*. That single objective has been so hard-wired into the DNA of wild creatures that it is still evident in the wolf descendants that have not tracked down an elk or a buffalo in hundreds of years.

Survival in business is often a matter of striking the right balance between risk and reward. I remember commenting years ago to one of my more daring business partners, "You're so used to living near the edge of the cliff that you think it's your backyard." Some folks in the investment business betray an easy comfort with risk, a carefree ability to let it dissolve in the recesses of their minds as they pursue the sumptuous rewards of our trade. But it was never easy for me. I was always preoccupied with the risk—but I was also stimulated by it. For me, the realm of private equity was both a precarious place to be and a natural place to be. It was certainly natural in the literal sense, since every day in the wild is spent on the edge, along the narrow precipice that separates success from failure.

There is something mesmerizing about watching creatures not just survive but *thrive* in that environment— mastering the challenges that abound in their universe. And then you stop and stare at your own reflection and realize how much you have in common with those four-legged creatures. It dawns on you that you are kindred spirits, for you too have survived—and thrived—in the precarious worlds you sought out for your own existence. I left the safety net of partnership in a prestigious law firm for the high-wire act of venture capital—and survived a series of tumbles in that world but thrived in the knowledge gained on the way down. Then I entered the world of leveraged buyouts when it was really not a world at all but only a shaky toehold on a new frontier. And after claiming my stake in that new frontier, I paused to take stock of covered ground and miles passed . . . and craved the feeling of being on the edge again. So I decided to become a wildlife photographer, apprenticing in a jeep and graduating to open helicopters to find a new perspective on my subjects down below. And I survived those flights of fantasy and experienced a very different sense of thriving when National Geographic published a trilogy of my aerial work.

Along the way, I bumped into a real threat to my survival when physicians discovered a defect in the structure of my heart. But I survived a trio of heart operations and then somehow managed to find a zone of rhythmic beating that doctors thought would never be mine again.

At the age of sixty-four, I put my cameras down, for I had taken the measure of myself in that world and thought it time to move on. But I missed being on the edge, for by then it had indeed become my backyard. So I went out and bought my first Harley and learned to cruise alongside motorcycles piloted by bikers born almost half a century after me. And it all felt right.

Preface

But I never take it for granted, not the financial security or the newfound health or even cruising the highways on my cycle. And I stare at those four-legged creatures who thrive along the narrow edge every day in Africa and even the ones with collars who harken back to a time when their ancestors did long ago. And I tip my hat in appreciation, for those four-legged professors have taught me much about surviving and thriving, secrets that I may tuck inside my three-piece suit or my safari vest or my biker jacket and use as my compass to navigate in a very precarious world.

Introduction

Four-Legged Professors

If you live among wolves, you have to act like a wolf.

—Nikita S. Khrushchev,
former premier of the Soviet Union

WHEN I WAS JUST A BOY, KHRUSHCHEV'S
blunt warning to Western diplomats at a reception in the
Polish embassy that "We will bury you!" was taken so
literally that its repetition in the press roused hairs on the
back of my neck.

With his bulbous face and rotund physique,
Khrushchev never inspired the glistening romance of an
elegantly dressed and coiffed Kennedy, but the portly Soviet
leader was spot on in his assessment of how to survive
among predators, be it in politics or business: *you must learn
to think and act like a predator.* Inside that hairless (but not
feckless) head, the Soviet premier possessed a psyche that
had absorbed the core lesson of survival in the natural world
and applied it to *his* realm, the domain of Russian politics.

The Stalinist era, in which Khrushchev not only
survived but managed to insinuate himself to the top of

1

a blood-soaked heap, was a dog-eat-dog theater of the grim. One false step and you were never heard from again, banished to a Siberian gulag where an occasional snowball fight was the only recreational activity on the agenda.

Khrushchev's words offer a priceless glimpse into the secrets of thriving in any hazardous field of endeavor: *focus on the survivors.* His choice of wolves was particularly fitting since the lessons may be gleaned not only from the long-fanged predators in the wild but also their more domesticated descendants who now sport collars and leashes.

The world of commerce, while hazardous in its own right, may appear to be a far cry from the brutality of the African plains. Even the dress codes of Wall Street and the savannah have nothing in common—except for the possibility of acquiring a Ralph Lauren suit at the same shop where you can purchase a designer safari outfit. But survival in business—fiscal rather than physical—is nevertheless a hard-hearted contest of endurance and strategy that, like its counterpart in the wild, is governed by few rules and even fewer referees. In the fiercely competitive domain of commerce, predators abound and prey is limited.

While scores of elite graduate schools and countless business manuals attempt to unravel the secrets to thriving in the world of commerce, it is rare that any of the pundits train their lens on the habits of our four-legged brethren. Gleaning business lessons from the wild creatures of Africa—let alone from a pack of mutts—is hardly considered standard fare for the apprentice programs at investment banks.

Indeed, the creatures that roam the few remaining outposts of undisturbed wilderness inhabit a world of raw instinct and physical prowess, where the cerebral artistry that powers the engines of commerce might seem to be wholly out of place. And a continent away from the grasslands of Africa, the moguls who operate in business would appear to have nothing to learn from the mongrels that coalesce into a unit of canine clanship. But the realms of two-legged businessmen and four-legged creatures are not nearly so foreign from each other as we might think. There are secrets to surviving in the wild that parallel the secrets to thriving in the slightly less brutish world of business.

With the benefit of more than twenty photo safaris deep into the recesses of Africa, I absorbed more of its lessons than I ever thought possible when I first inhaled the continent's distinctive scents. The bushveld is not merely a throwback to a region that thrived in more distant times. It is a dynamic organism where the themes of life and death, mating and procreation, defending precious territory, and assuring future lineage play out constantly in an ever-evolving drama in which there are treasured secrets to thriving.

In extracting business lessons from the savannah grasslands of Africa—and the more manicured lawns on which our pups hold sway—we would do well to think of the landscape as props and the creatures as characters in a play from which we may absorb teachings that can be transported from one theater to another. It is the plot itself and not the props or the costumes that matters most. Otherwise, there would be no point in attending a performance of *Hamlet*, lest we be distracted by the wind-swept castle at Elsinore or Danish men in tights and miss altogether the timeless lessons that Shakespeare infused in his plot—about treachery, revenge, self-doubt, and corruption.

Virtually all the major tasks that must be overcome in the world of commerce have an analogy in the wild: the setting of sensible goals, the conservation of precious resources, the astute decision making that is a constant challenge, the definition of territorial rights, the judicious use of time, and even the ability to distinguish between the spoils of victory and becoming spoiled by victory. It all plays out in the four-legged world.

There is something valuable to be learned from any species that has survived for thousands of years. Sheer size and strength alone could not possibly be the code to survival or else we would still be bumping into saber-toothed tigers and woolly mammoths on our way to the grocery store. Instead, there are more subtle secrets at work in the ability of certain creatures to span the ages from prehistoric times to the present, true masters of their universe. And the more I studied those creatures with sophisticated camera gadgetry in Africa—or even the wolf descendants in my own backyard—the more those secrets revealed their hidden meaning.

In our knee-jerk embrace of newfangled contraptions that abound in an increasingly complex world, we have lost our appetite for the simple things that form the keel of a more balanced life. We have become enamored with the devices that intrude into every crevice of our existence and force the spinning carousel of daily life to accelerate to the point where we often lose our sense of perspective. And that perspective is so difficult to regain without stepping off the carousel.

A photographic safari among the predators of the Masai Mara takes place in a mystical realm where there are no carousels, and so does an hour-long walk with a pack of mutts around the edge of a duck-filled pond. Forays into the wilderness permit us to step away from the fray long enough to observe the more straightforward lessons taught by four-legged professors for whom English is a foreign tongue. And once we observe those lessons in action, we marvel at how the secrets may be transported back to the world of commerce (and even the broader domain of our daily lives) once we set foot upon the carousel again. Simple secrets all, that lend credence to the fact that we would do well to heed the lessons taught by the four-legged professors who are indeed masters of their universe.

Masters of Their Universe

Chapter One

Decisions, Decisions, Decisions

Masters of Their Universe

Secret #1

When in doubt,
make the more correctable mistake

Masters of Their Universe

When you come to a fork in the road, take it.

—Yogi Berra,
Hall of Fame catcher for the New York Yankees

YOGI WAS A GREAT CATCHER AND A DARN
good satirist, but not exactly a fount of wisdom when it
came to applying the art of baseball to the world of business.
There may well be a brilliant nugget embedded somewhere
in his pithy comment about forks in the road, but it certainly
is well camouflaged. It's as if Yogi took us to the most vital
intersection along the thoroughfare of business—if not life
itself—and then just left us standing there with our hands
in our pockets while the Yankee legend sauntered away
chuckling to himself.

But at least Yogi did lead us to the right place—
forks in the road, conundrums, dilemmas—all just other
names for points of key decision making. And good decision
making is what it's all about in business—that plus a strong
dose of luck. Since we have no control over when or how
the fickle crosscurrents of commerce may steer a hefty wave
of luck our way, we'd be well advised to sharpen the power
of good decision making as we journey through the choppy
waters of business.

The More Correctable Mistake

Often, we are prone to rely on time-worn adages such as "Just follow your gut instinct when it comes to a tough decision." Good advice . . . assuming there is such a thing as "gut instinct" and that if there is, your gut is not torn between two choices that appear to be equally appealing. It sounds like such a fantastically attractive trait to have—like deep blue eyes set below a head of curly dark hair (think Paul Newman)—that geneticists should be hard at work cloning creatures with impeccable gut instinct. Regrettably, or thankfully, genetic engineering has not yet advanced to that level of sophistication. So if we are to rely on a trusty adage to steer us in the right direction every time we come to Yogi's proverbial fork in the road, we would be well served to have some other pearl of wisdom to rely on.

The brightest person I ever met in business was a fellow named Alfred Lerner. When I was a first-year associate at a Cleveland law firm, the managing partner, Jim Berick, assigned me to a sequence of complex transactions in which Al was the client. Fresh out of law school, I may not have had any practical experience, but I knew enough to appreciate the wisdom of the saying "Hitch your wagon to a star." Al was not just any star; this man was a budding rock star of business playing to fairly small crowds along the shores of Lake Erie. So I attached myself to him with as much Velcro as I could. I volunteered for every assignment—large or small—that had anything to do with the empire that Al was in the process of assembling.

This Brooklyn native and son of Russian immigrants lived above his parents' candy shop as a youngster, eventually attending Columbia University and then serving as a pilot in the US Marine Corps. By the time I met Al in 1972, his marine uniform had been closeted for quite a few years in favor of impeccable suits and spit-polished shoes. A Cuban cigar—lit or unlit—roughly the size of a redwood sapling was always in his hand or his mouth. Over the course of the next three decades, Al amassed a fortune in real estate and finance, bought the Cleveland Browns NFL franchise for more than $500 million, served as president of the world-renowned Cleveland Clinic Foundation, and donated huge sums of money to charitable endeavors.

When I first met Al, the building blocks of his eventual empire were only in the early stages, but his larger-than-life swagger and brutally incisive intellect were already on vivid display, whether we were in negotiations together or just caucusing privately. I immediately fell in love with him, as a mentor and a father figure. And I never lost that affection for him, even after his tragic death from a brain tumor at the age of sixty-nine. The only explanation I can think of for Al's early death from a disease that attacked his peerless brain is that a higher power must have craved the comfort of having this man with his titanic intellect sitting right beside him rather than operating in the world down below.

The words of wisdom that I inherited from Al— always laced with a tart dose of Brooklyn sarcasm—were the perfect boots-on-the-ground complement to my classroom schooling at Yale and Harvard Law. Seated beside him in setting after setting in which decision making was a nonstop exercise, I was captivated by his ability to make rapid-fire choices whenever we encountered a fork in the road—and mesmerized by the nearly flawless quality of his decisions.

One day I asked him outright about his uncanny ability to make the right judgment call. Al twirled the lubricated end of his cigar around in his lips and then bestowed upon me the most valuable piece of advice I have ever received: "When in doubt, make the more correctable mistake." Expanded on a bit, that advice would translate roughly as follows: when you come to a fork in the road, weigh both options carefully and imagine the harm of being wrong in each of your two possible choices; then select the path that causes the least damage if it turns out to have been the wrong choice.

There is a certain breadth to this insight that is not confined to the playing field of business: *Not sure whether to marry someone?* Then wait—it will be easier to pop the question in a few months than it will be to extract yourself from marital vows that should never have been exchanged in the first place. *Not sure whether you're ready to have your first child?* Then hold off on expanding your family—raising children is tough enough when you never have to doubt whether you should have had that child in the first place.

The number of times that I've employed Al's maxim about "the more correctable mistake" is countless. It is the precious inheritance that I received from this man whom I think of often and miss dearly.

Unforgivable Mistakes
Imagine what the world of business would be like if every time you made a wrong decision, you not only lost your money but you also lost your life. The vacancy rate for office space on Wall Street would skyrocket to unprecedented levels, and prime rental property in the business district would be there for the taking at $10 per square foot. The only businesspeople still walking around would be the

survivors with unerring judgment.

Not so incredibly, there is such a world out there, populated with creatures that would just as soon munch on someone wearing an Hermes tie as sit down and sip a latte with him. In that domain, you lose more than worldly goods when you guess wrong. In the wild—and deep within the DNA that has been handed down to canines from their gray wolf ancestors—survival at the end of the day is the only measuring stick that counts.

Creatures in the African bush rely on a potent blend of instinct and cognitive reasoning carried out in a theater in which the script has no preordained endings. When it comes to survival, that combination of instinct and reasoning is in many ways more highly developed than the ones we hominids possess. The instinctual side of their functioning in the wild has been honed over generations by some type of survival manual that was implanted in their genes and then slightly modified as each new generation passed its wisdom down to the next. By definition, the species that are still walking around out there have made plenty of savvy decisions when their ancestors reached countless forks in the road.

Contrary to popular belief, predators in the wild are not profligate risk-takers, but rather more risk-averse unless life is at stake. Once the creator of Africa decided not to install grocery stores in the pristine plains of the Masai Mara, predators had no choice but to engage in mortal combat to survive, both in hunting forays and by carving up the African turf into territorial fiefdoms to be defended to the death. In those fiefdoms, hunting missions and territorial squabbles are not undertaken without carefully weighing the risks and the rewards that are at stake.

Even a four-hundred-pound lion will eventually succumb to the collateral damage from a zebra's bucking kick that fractures its jaw or a buffalo horn that pierces its stomach. The horns and hooves of those seemingly docile herbivores have been known to be the undoing of the carnivorous master of the plains. I once witnessed a young, careless male lion stray too far inside the fringes of a buffalo herd that the lion and his cohorts were stalking. The intruder was soon surrounded by a dozen or so snorting bovines, heads lowered and hooves positioned to trample and gore to death their enemy. The lion disappeared from view within a cadre of buffalos in what was certain to be his last and most painful lesson in the perils of confrontation. Seconds later, I was stunned to see the lion's body somersaulting through the air out of the circle of death, when one of his tormenters mistakenly tossed him to freedom with a flip of its massive horned head. The dazed lion staggered away with wounds that would be a lasting reminder that lion-buffalo skirmishes are a deadly *two-way* stretch of road.

As a group of lions surveys a herd of zebras moseying across rich grasslands, they are attempting to figure out the optimal circumstances that favor an attack. If those circumstances do not unfold to their liking, the lions will normally back off and make the more correctable mistake— passing up a potential meal of zebra tartare is certainly more correctable than launching a reckless attack that leaves the hunter with a broken jaw or an injured limb that may prove fatal.

But in the wild—as in the canyons of Wall Street— the more correctable mistake does not always equate to backing away from a confrontation. If it did, there would be an awful lot of very skinny predators out there. I once watched a female cheetah skirmish with a pair of much larger males that were intent on implanting her with the seeds of future lineage and were not inclined to take "no" for an answer. On the surface, her choosing to give in to a bit of romantic coupling would seem to have been more correctable (if a mistake at all) than engaging in fisticuffs with those two brutes. But she knew exactly what she was doing, and her decision to scuffle with the amorous males was considerably more reasoned than simply not being in the mood.

In a grove of trees only about one hundred yards away, the female had hidden four young cubs that might well have been casualties along the fringes of this adult skirmish. Clearly, the female was protecting her cubs by wandering away with the two males in tow. But even more interesting, somewhere deep within her feline psyche, the cheetah mother probably realized that having a second litter of cubs while attempting to raise the first was an impossible task, where the nearly inevitable outcome would have been starvation or violent death for all concerned.

In the brief scuffle that ensued among the three adult cheetahs, there was snarling and swiping and lunging but no visible injury at all. The female had two risky choices, and she opted for the path that avoided almost certain death for herself and her brood, even though it involved a confrontation with two hefty and horny males. She did indeed choose the more correctable mistake.

Years ago while on safari, I jotted down a journal entry that paid tribute to the creatures that manage to avoid the unforgivable mistake:

Last night I slept in my blue long johns, but I left the doors to my deck wide open. Despite the cold, I wanted to hear the low groan of the lion, the plaintive howl of the hyena, and the angry bark of the baboon, as if to say: "We are still here! The drama continues even as you sleep, even when your camera is in its case, even when you no longer return to Africa. This drama of ours needs no audience, the roles are passed from generation to generation like an artisan's craft, but the script changes every day and every night. We need no critic's review to know how well we did. If we show up for work tomorrow, we did well."

The Deal Best Left for Others

True to their wolf heritage, the Haas clan of mixed breeds has its fair share of intramural squabbles, since the seat of power is a much-coveted position that subjects the alpha male to a gauntlet of recurrent challenges. Although conflicts within our band of mutts occasionally escalate to the point where fur will fly, more often than not fang-bearing growls give way to one of the guys rolling over on his back, exposing a soft underbelly to his more dominant opponent, and the victor walking away after one last triumphant stare. Each combatant has chosen to make the "more correctable mistake" that its wolf relatives often make. For the submissive wolf, surrender is a more prudent path than potentially mortal combat. And for the dominant one, walking away with its leadership intact and its body unscathed is clearly more advisable than killing one of its pack members and risking injury in the process. The leaders realized long ago that one bloody confrontation after another would ultimately thin the ranks of a wolf clan that was best served by having a full battalion of able-bodied hunters.

Despite the pin-striped wrapping, almost every conundrum of decision making in the business world is a distant cousin of the fight-or-flight dilemma that dominates the world of four-legged creatures. Not every fight is one to be taken on when you amble about on four legs, and not every deal is one to be made when you only have two.

The private equity world has no more critical setting in which to apply the sage advice of making the more correctable mistake than in the conference room where a group of partners sit with sleeves rolled up, deciding whether or not to move forward with a deal that has been thoroughly researched and heavily negotiated. By that point, exhaustive due diligence of the target company's pros and cons has exposed the hidden weaknesses that lie beneath its more obvious strengths, its senior management has been subjected to rigorous scrutiny, and the contours of an industry with which you were barely familiar just a couple of months earlier have become more distinct. There you sit with the ultimate decision in the hands of a few partners who must signal "thumbs up" or "thumbs down" on moving forward.

Sometimes, there is hardly any uncertainty at all; the intensive investigation has only served to confirm your initial positive reaction and heighten your conviction that this company is destined to be part of your portfolio. But often, your stomach is queasier than you thought it would be at this critical juncture, and you go around the table ping-ponging the arguments for and against the investment. I have been in that setting dozens of times—and whenever the arguments appear to be evenly balanced, I can hear (and often will vocalize) Al's advice that we make the more correctable mistake.

Walking away from a deal that might in fact turn out to be a good one is certainly more correctable than making an investment you wish you had never made. If you walk away from a deal that in retrospect you should have made, at least you still have all your funds in your pocket ready to be deployed in the next deal. But if you sink your money into an ill-advised investment, it's awfully hard to extract your capital from the sticky briar patch of a bad deal. On the many occasions when it has been a close call, the precept of the more correctable mistake has normally held sway, and we have snapped our briefcases shut and headed for the exit.

I often think about the fact that the least publicized good decisions in the investment business are the deals that we choose *not* to do—the ones that would have been devastating if we had moved forward. Dodging disaster is an invaluable skill in business just as in the wild. As my grandpa Arthur once told me, "You never go broke from a deal you don't do." Arthur never met Al, but each one managed to make the more correctable mistake over and over again.

Chapter Two

Searching for Pay Dirt

Masters of Their Universe

Secret #2

Life is a contact sport,
so stay focused on the end zone

Masters of Their Universe

Give me a stock clerk with a goal and
I'll give you a man who will make history.
Give me a man with no goals and I'll give you a stock clerk.

—James Cash Penney,
founder of J.C. Penney department stores

IN THE COURSE OF ALMOST FOUR DECADES
in the world of finance, I have found that the most successful men and women do not have very complex goals, but relatively simple ones that are capable of clear recitation and straight-line execution. It was a phenomenon that the retailing maestro James Cash Penney understood so well.

Staying focused on the so-called end zone of your professional life is critical to ending up on that sacred turf—you rarely land there by accident. But to stay focused on the end zone, you must *first* decide what it's supposed to look like, what it is that you're chasing. Defining why you do what you do is indispensable to achieving your goals. Otherwise you are merely a blur of pumping arms and legs heading at breakneck speed toward a place of indeterminate value.

The Art of Bank Robbery

Whether exaggerated or not, the famous gangster William "Willie" Sutton is reputed to have once answered a reporter's question as to why he robbed banks with the classic line, "Because that's where the money is." Credited with pilfering more than $2 million from roughly one hundred banks during his brilliant thirty-year career, Willie selected a profession for which he had a natural aptitude, and he obviously knew exactly why he did what he did. Despite all the pitfalls and dangers, Sutton was steadfast in his pursuit of the one career that always captured his imagination, undeterred by a few "rest periods" along the way as a guest at several of our more renowned penitentiaries. Undistracted by extraneous goals and career hand-wringing, Sutton was free to adorn his professional résumé with a reputation for witticisms and a penchant for stylish clothes that endeared him to both the Mafioso dons and the public at large.

Lest we think that Sutton's quip about knowing exactly why he robbed banks is nothing more than a humorous anecdote from the lips of a career criminal, his retort about "that's where the money is" is actually credited as the genesis for Sutton's Law, taught in medical schools as the recommended approach of going straight to the most obvious diagnosis of an ailment.

In more modern times, genius entrepreneurs— operating within the bounds of propriety that Sutton found so constrictive—have converted straightforward visions into economic juggernauts by mixing *focus* with *creativity*—Steve Jobs in the ever-evolving world of personal computing and Mark Zuckerberg in the nearly ubiquitous realm of social networking. Penney, Jobs, Zuckerberg—complex men who nurtured simple visions with laser-like focus. In each case, it all began with the rather basic notion of defining one's ambition and then never losing sight of the end zone. The formula is the same, regardless of how lofty or how grounded that ambition may be.

Predators and the Rules of the Energy Bank

For almost two decades, I have patiently observed the behavior of predators, and our four-legged friends seem to understand much better than we do the importance of staying focused on a clearly defined goal. With single-minded purpose, adult predators dedicate their precious resources to the well-defined goal of *survival*—staking out and protecting turf where prey are plentiful, engaging in the life-and-death drama of hunting, and mating in order to assure their continued lineage.

The hunters in the wild know full well where the "end zone" of their career lies. Everything they do is geared toward that one paramount goal. By definition, the species that are still walking around out there are highly focused and exceptionally good at their craft.

There may not be much career choice for wild predators, but there *is* the option of how they spend their time when they're not tracking prey or giving chase. And the reality is that the vast majority of that time is spent resting, an activity that consumes the least amount of energy while restoring strength and vitality. In between bursts of hunting, mating, or fighting, adult lions can be seen just lying around grooming, yawning, and snoring for up to twenty hours a day.

Four-legged hunters waste virtually no time or

calories in frivolous activities that are not directly related to their survival. On the surface, the carefree antics of the young may seem like an exception, but lion cubs have plenty of extra energy to burn, and even playful wrestling is a way to hone fighting skills and establish relative clan position. The only institutional law in the wild is the rule by which the Energy Bank operates: *Life consists solely of making deposits into and withdrawals from your account at this bank. The intake of food and water are your deposits, and the energy expended moving around, fighting, and hunting are your withdrawals. You may remain a customer of this bank so long as your account is never overdrawn.*

As prudent customers of the Energy Bank, the predators of Africa know full well that a key ingredient in the recipe of remaining focused is knowing when "enough is enough" and how not to be sidetracked by extraneous pursuits. The goal is survival, not knocking off as many impalas as possible. Conquering for the sake of conquest— just like buying for the sake of owning—is an elusive goal that has no natural end zone. If a cheetah chases an impala merely for the sake of the chase even though it is not hungry, that cheetah is just wasting precious energy. Regardless of whether the hoofed object of its fascination is a 120-pound impala or a diminutive 11-pound dik-dik, a cheetah has only one driving, instinctual ambition at work when it begins to stalk its prey: *survival.* In close to twenty years of photographing wild creatures, I have yet to see a successful hunt where the predator just left the carcass lying on the ground uneaten.

Whether in business or on the African savannah, if you are consumed with the sheer thrill of hunting rather than the underlying rationale for the hunt, you have embarked on a journey toward an end zone where the goalposts will forever shift; no matter how bloated your belly or how robust your bank account, there's always another impala whizzing by.

The Great Migration: Focus in the Face of Adversity

The advantage of staying focused on a clearly defined goal is not limited to one side of the finely tuned balance between predator and prey. The herds that roam this theater of confrontation appreciate the lesson just as well.

The most impressive spectacle of single-minded pursuit that I have ever witnessed is the Great Migration of wildebeest and other ungulates that circumnavigate the Masai Mara and Serengeti grasslands every year in search of fertile pastures and abundant water. It is an odyssey that exacts a fearsome toll on legions of their members. Hundreds of thousands of the herbivores succumb to hunger, thirst, exhaustion, and predation, none more spectacularly than the wildebeest brought down by a flotilla of crocodiles that awaits their crossing of the Grumeti River in Tanzania and the Mara River in Kenya. It is a humbling sight to behold—a drama that unfolds without script or special effects, elevating the woefully inadequate words *focus* and *adversity* to unimaginable levels.

Career Choice: The Long and Winding Road

For predators in the wild, there's really not much career choice—you either hunt or you die. By contrast, it stands to reason that we should know exactly why we endure the arduous schooling and apprenticeship for any vocation, why we select one career path over another, why we change careers in midstream, and why we keep marching along the potholed road of our chosen profession. But the fact of the matter is that an awful lot of people seem to be stumped for an answer when asked *exactly* why they're on the path they're on and where it's supposed to lead.

With a medical file that has the girth of the Gutenberg Bible and a troop of aging canines with their own long list of ailments, I spend a fair amount of time with my own physicians and with a bevy of veterinarians. There's an interesting phenomenon that I've noticed when I chat with these professionals about their careers. Even though the demanding schooling and the rigors of residency and practice are similar for both types of physicians, the reactions I get when I probe as to why they do what they do are noticeably different. The human physicians tend to mumble something along the lines of "that's what I was trained to do" or just stare at me with a blank expression as if the question were posed in an ancient Celtic dialect that bears only a glancing resemblance to English. Often those doctors confess to an acute sense of disillusionment—almost a feeling of betrayal that all the hassles of insurance forms and health care regulations and malpractice suits have sapped their original motivation for entering the noble profession of healing others. But the vets—who earn only a fraction of their human-physician counterparts—answer with almost precisely the same words: "Because I love to heal animals." Even the older, more experienced veterinarians respond with a palpable sense of passion for their craft. It's almost as if that very passion for healing has acted as a booster fuel to keep their career focus intact, undiminished by the long hours and the constant setbacks of lost patients along the way. It is simply single-minded focus on a well-defined career goal. They are modern-day Willie Suttons with white coats and stethoscopes, rather than a mask and a pistol.

It's one thing to experiment early on in our careers with one course and then switch to another or to be unsure what the end zone is supposed to look like until it comes into sharper focus. But it's something else to just wander around in the wilderness without a map in our backpacks. The end zone need not be of headline-grabbing notoriety in order to be worthy of our deepest admiration—I have great respect for the firefighter or the coal miner who says, "This is all I ever wanted to do. . . . My father and his father before him were firefighters [coal miners], and it's just in my blood." The certainty that lies beneath that comment is admirable, and the men and women who utter it, despite all the dangers and sacrifices inherent in their jobs, know exactly why they don their uniform every morning. Beneath that uniform, there is indeed a single-minded focus on a well-defined goal.

In my case, a rocky childhood was a great boon in terms of helping me to define my own personal quest. After abandoning a privileged but oppressive home life as a rebellious teenager in favor of a spartan boarding house and a series of makeshift abodes after that, I eventually matured enough to come to grips with exactly what I was looking for. I had left financial security behind when I deserted a dysfunctional family home, and in the years that followed, I trained my sights on replacing it with a security of my own making. At some point along the way, I realized that if my efforts proved to be successful, I would also be exchanging a wounded self-esteem for one that would be better fortified against the battering that life has in store for all of us.

As my career route ricocheted from law to venture capital to leveraged buyouts, the shape of the playing field may have morphed from courthouse to conference room, but the contours of the end zone never changed. The goal was still long-term financial security. In my eyes, the hallmark of that fortress was always the ability to lock the office doors at night and never come back again, without compromising my lifestyle or the nest egg that I planned to set aside for my family. That way, if I *did* come back to the office the next morning, it would be because I *wanted* to, not because I *had* to.

At times, this self-imposed target felt like a heavy burden to bear, for that is the very nature of ambition, but that target nevertheless guided me forward. And when I eventually reached the end zone after only a handful of years in the leveraged buyout business, the simple patch of grass beneath my feet felt good. It felt like I belonged there, and I had no intention of leaving it ever again.

Mileposts vs. Goalposts

Part of the challenge of staying focused on a career objective is the ability to recognize the critical difference between interim *mileposts* and the ultimate *goalpost*. I never once saw a cheetah celebrate at the side of a fallen impala. Bringing that impala down was simply one step forward on its path toward long-term survival. Within the next few days and for every week that followed, the cheetah would need to pass a fresh milepost—having outsprinted and tripped up another foe—or else its ultimate goal of long-term survival would be in jeopardy.

And so it is in the world of private equity. Closing a single deal was never my ultimate goal. It was simply a milepost along the long march forward. Each deal in the portfolio of a private equity practitioner is one building block in the process of constructing the cozy abode of long-term security—and no one throws a housewarming party for a partially completed home.

I have often noticed how the most renowned coaches in the annals of sports also seem to be the ones who were best able to distinguish between mere mileposts and the Holy Grail of achieving lifetime ambition. In the realm of professional football, the Holy Grail is the Super Bowl (or perhaps induction into the Hall of Fame), whereas scoring a single touchdown is a feat that is accomplished well over a thousand times each year in the pigskin world. The greatest coaches in the history of the National Football League—luminaries such as Paul Brown of the Cleveland Browns and Vince Lombardi of the Green Bay Packers—were also among the ones least tolerant of the impromptu celebrations that sometimes erupt on the field when a player crosses the goal line. Brown reportedly admonished his team, "When you reach the end zone, act like you've been there before."

Growing up in the 1950s along the shores of Lake Erie, I still recall vivid images of one of Coach Brown's disciples, Hall of Fame running back Jim Brown, casually dropping the football or gently handing it off to the nearest referee after a touchdown. You could almost read his mind at such blasé moments, as if to say, "Well, of course, that's what I was supposed to do all along." The only time I ever saw the gap-toothed Lombardi smile was when he was hoisted on the shoulders of his victorious charges after the Packers garnered another of their many league championships. Except for those end-of-season festivities, Lombardi's face was normally stony and expressionless.

Brown and Lombardi instilled in their teams the value of distinguishing between the transitory trip that a single touchdown affords into the end zone on a playing field and the ultimate goal of achieving the pinnacle in your chosen field. Both coaches would undoubtedly have been appalled by the post-touchdown antics of today's NFL players, which more closely resemble a bad tryout for the TV show *Dancing with the Stars* than they do a mature professional athlete achieving one step forward in moving toward a career goal.

It was a simpler era fifty years ago when I was a youngster, one in which a person defined his or her career objectives early on and was expected to march toward those goals in straight-line fashion, without a lot of fanfare or bellyaching along the way. There was hardly any confusion between mileposts and goalposts, and little celebration until the latter were reached. I carried that mind-set with me onto the campuses of the schools I attended, into the swimming pools where I competed, and eventually into the professions I chose to pursue. Perhaps it was the psychic bruises from a tough childhood or the fear that all the good fortune could be swept away if I lost my focus, but I never quite figured out how (or why) to celebrate the passage of individual mileposts. The goal of financial security still lay ahead, and that was the only marker that counted.

Savoring the Moment

If I were to pinpoint the one wildlife image that comes most readily to mind as a moment of triumph, it would be that of a panting cheetah standing breathless at the side of a fallen impala brought down after a race for the ages between the most fleet-footed of predator and prey. The cheetah has focused on its target, it has engaged in battle, and it has prevailed. But it is also wary—scanning the horizon for signs that a larger predator might come along at any moment to snatch the prize it has captured. For like monetary security, the cheetah's bounty is never truly permanent. It is to be savored in the moment but must be jealously guarded against the risk of being forfeited.

Masters of Their Universe

Chapter Three

Gazing in the Mirror

Masters of Their Universe

Secret #3

*Know your weaknesses
as well as you know your strengths*

Masters of Their Universe

Good sex is like good bridge. If you don't have a good partner,
you'd better have a good hand.

—Mae West,
American actress, playwright, and sex symbol

NOTORIOUS GODDESS OF THE BROADWAY

stage and the silver screen, Mae West packed a bawdy wit and prickly intellect inside her voluptuous but diminutive five-foot frame. Although her amorous adventures reputedly crossed over the line into bigamy with a pair of marriages that may have overlapped for a mere six years or so, Mae knew a thing or two about partnering. As graphically illustrated in the quote above, she realized that without a good partner, you have no one to count on but yourself . . . and private equity is a rough neighborhood to roam around in without a mate.

In business as in life itself, the importance of a good partner is often overlooked as a vital ingredient in the recipe for success. The journals of the day and the investment community trumpet the exploits of *individuals* (Buffett, Gates, Kravis, Zuckerberg) rather than their unsung colleagues. Individuals—and the vivid details of both their escapades and their indiscretions—simply make for better tabloid fodder than partnerships. After all, only individuals—and not partnerships—are capable of such noteworthy feats as springing back from being a college dropout or taking on a third trophy wife or purchasing a shower curtain for $16,000.

The analogies to sex and bridge are even more to the point than Ms. West may have ever imagined. In business as with sex, it is the assets of one partner dovetailing with the assets of the other that creates the inherent genius of the bond. And just as in the game of bridge where no one comes to the table with fifty-two cards in their hand, the ability of business partners to forge an alliance that complements their respective strengths and compensates for their inevitable weaknesses is what fashions a winning hand.

We all enter the arena of business with glaring gaps that are best filled by others. After all, we may be masterful at certain things, but no one is masterful at everything. It is only by recognizing those gaps—*knowing the things that we're bad at*—and filling those shortcomings with the talents of a compatible partner that we ferret out the ultimate strength of the alliance.

The Limits of Our Prowess

The leopard is sometimes referred to as the consummate predator of Africa. This exotic blend of stealth and grace earned its reputation in part because it normally covers the night shift as one of the few nocturnal hunters and in part because it prefers to work alone. However, the solitary leopard is the exception to the rule; the majority of predators that roam the African continent do so in tandem with their compatriots. Lioness hunting parties may actually adopt relay or divide-and-conquer strategies to bring down prey, while hyenas bunch together in a fearsome horde that may even try its hand at poaching from a lion feasting on the fruits of a successful hunt. While the climax of a coordinated clan assault on the intended target is often followed by self-centered squabbling over the fallen carcass, the net result is that the partners will ultimately share in the kill and thus benefit from the strength of their union. Their power lies in coalition, their vulnerability in isolation.

Pack animals roam with their clan mates not merely for the sake of kinship, but because that very kinship and the dynamics of the group serve to cover up their weaknesses. Weighing in at a mere forty to sixty pounds, an individual African wild dog boasts neither the brawn nor jaw strength to bring down a 250-pound hartebeest or even a 120-pound impala, let alone protect that size of a kill from larger predators. But as part of a marauding band of ten or twenty, wild dogs are more than equal to the task. With an almost inexhaustible reservoir of endurance, wild dogs give chase to much larger and faster prey, confident that their quarry will eventually succumb to exhaustion and the clan will prevail.

In the Okavango Delta of Botswana, I once photographed a pack of wild dogs stalking a large herd of impalas, which splintered into a hasty three-pronged retreat once the attack began. Almost as if it had been choreographed, the wild dog pack immediately divided itself into three divisions, each giving chase to one of the three groups of fleeing impalas. Eventually each wild dog troop brought down an impala, and the frenzied feast began in earnest. Even in their moment of triumph, the wild dogs protected their bounty from their own shortcomings—by disemboweling their capture in a matter of minutes, the mob left virtually nothing to be poached by larger predators.

Clanship—the raw math of like-minded partners who provide heft to the team—is only one way in which African predators compensate for their own limitations. In a stunning display of head-and-neck strength and climbing prowess, a solitary leopard is capable of hoisting a fresh kill equal to its own weight straight up a tree in order to stash its quarry across branches that are out of range of lion and hyena competitors. The leopard's legendary ambush skills have brought down its quarry, and its equally impressive ability to haul that hard-earned prize up a tree makes up for its inability to defend its catch on the ground from more powerful predators. Even the proverbial king of beasts knows its own limitations. While lions will pursue much larger prey across open plains, their bravado usually ends at water's edge—I have seen many a lion growl and snarl helplessly at this point, knowing that ponds and rivers mark the end of their territory and the beginning of the domain where crocodiles reign supreme. Below sea level, the lion is no match for a croc that may drag it down to a watery grave.

Slotting Strengths with Weaknesses

I emerged from my youth with a noticeably truncated set of social skills, no doubt the result of having left home at an early age. Exceedingly cautious and suspicious, I was quick to anger and slow to trust. That is hardly a prescription for developing the kind of robust network of social and business contacts on which young lawyers depend for new clients and investors depend for deal flow. To succeed in either profession, I needed to adopt a different strategy from the classic network of contacts woven by my peers—to say the least, my web of relationships was several notches shy of six degrees of separation.

During the barrister phase of my professional life, rather than attempting to become the social animal I was not by casting a wide net for potential clients, I decided to wedge my way onto the legal teams that represented the firm's largest corporate clients. Relieved for the time being from the pressures of attracting fresh business to the firm, I routinely billed more hours than any of my peers and soared to the top of the list of young associates slated for promotion to partnership. But the clarion call of becoming a *principal* rather than an *advisor* was irresistible, and I resigned my freshly minted law partnership in favor of joining a Cleveland venture capital firm.

After a notably lackluster stint in venture capital, I decided that my destiny in the investment business did not reside along the shores of Lake Erie. But I also knew that it would be sheer folly to strike out on my own. So I shook hands with a tall and charismatic veteran of private equity by the name of Tom Hicks, and in 1984 we launched the Dallas-based buyout shop named, appropriately enough, Hicks & Haas.

On the surface, ours was an improbable partnership between a thirty-eight-year-old native Texan and a thirty-six-year-old from the suburbs of Cleveland. A Southerner with a nose for gushers and an Ivy-educated lawyer with a keen eye for the soft underbelly of risk. An amiable Mr. Outside with a dog-eared Rolodex and a vibrant network of priceless deal contacts, and a detail-obsessed and reclusive Mr. Inside with a flair for the intricacies of deal making and a relish for hard-nosed negotiating. We dovetailed perfectly in the sense that our strengths neatly complemented the other's weaknesses, all bonded together with a healthy respect and affection for each other and an awareness that we clearly needed what the other fellow brought to the party.

We were each "rainmakers" of a different sort. Tom was a storm chaser *par excellence*, and I knew where we had stashed the umbrellas. Hicks & Haas (and Messrs. Hicks and Haas) took on the swagger of a compact muscle car, in which one of the two senior partners had a heavy foot on the accelerator and the other on the brake. It was an exceedingly practical combination: without a gas pedal we would have gone nowhere, and without a brake we might have ended up as twisted wreckage.

The 1980s were a magical era in the history of private equity, when dazzling opportunities abounded and intense competition had not yet flocked to the fore. I have often described it as the Oklahoma land rush days of the leveraged buyout business when all you needed was a six-shooter, a covered wagon, and a team of freshly watered horses. But actually you needed something more—you needed a partner who could share the reins with you, who could tug left when you drifted too far to the right, who could spell you when fatigue blunted your reaction time, and who could share the blame when things went wrong. With Hicks & Haas, we found ourselves in the right place at the right time . . . and we each found the right partner to capitalize on the outsized opportunities that presented themselves. We both knew what we were good at and, more importantly, we knew what the other guy was better at.

We also knew that the nonstop tap-dance routine of sharing the top slot in a partnership is one that eventually leaves you rubbery legged unless you either call a halt to the music or figure out how to divvy up the limelight. Even in our earliest days, we each gravitated to the phases of the deal business that played to our own strengths and gave wide berth to the other fellow within the domain of his natural strengths. It was not a precise formula that dictated who should be taking on which task or chairing which meeting or when we should share the baton in a seamless display of unity. It was more a case of our both knowing—at times spoken and at times merely understood—what would be most effective in a particular setting, and we simply assumed our respective roles without colliding into each other. We were adept at saving our sharp elbows for negotiating with the parties on the other side and not nudging each other off the dais.

After a brief but heady joy ride in the leveraged buyout business, we decided to part ways in 1989 with a handshake and an embrace. For years afterward, we were often asked by the media and our cohorts in the trade why we would break up such an outlandishly profitable partnership. Respectful of what we each brought to the party, we often responded with something to the effect of, "There are three secrets to a great partnership: knowing who to partner with, knowing what to do after you open for business, and knowing when to call it quits. We were three for three."

Unplugged . . . But Still Flawed
Financial security, judiciously employed, can buy you time away from the maelstrom of business. Over the past two decades, I have chosen to fill that vacuum with my two-

legged and four-legged clans and with the passionate pursuit of photography and writing, each a form of retreating from the world at large. The boy who spent countless hours alone has become the man who finds private time to be well worth guarding from encroachment. In a world where connectivity is ubiquitous, I have discovered that there is no price tag to be placed on the value of being unconnected—roaming the African plains, floating in a helicopter over Arctic glaciers, or just strolling along the edges of a pond with my faithful companions.

After a quarter century in the investment business, retirement at one extreme and financial roadkills at the other have thinned the ranks of my contemporaries down to a handful who have risen to positions of prominence at powerful financial institutions. As surviving veterans of the 1980s who experienced the Oklahoma land rush days together, we still have a way of occasionally reaching out to each other to create alliances that capitalize on old relationships and take advantage of new investment opportunities.

Nevertheless, I continue to align myself with partners whose strengths compensate for my imbedded weaknesses. On the one hand, I am not at all reluctant to pit my negotiating skills or sense of bottom-line judgment against my colleagues in the trade. But on the other, the combination of my reclusive nature and aversion to investing time and energy into spinning an intricate web of contacts has never enabled me to jettison completely my reliance on others for the lifeblood of deal flow. My penchant for solitude has spawned a dependence on a certain type of partner who is more willing to barter his privacy in pursuit of our common aims. Like everything else we do inside (or outside) our offices, it is all a trade-off where the tongue-in-groove process of slotting strengths between weaknesses forms a bond whereby the clan is stronger than its individual members.

When I reflect on the LBO heyday of the 1980s and 1990s, I realize that our timing for entering the choppy waters of private equity was exquisitely fortuitous. Those pioneer days were littered with opportunity, and I managed to link up with an exceptionally talented partner whose persona melded just right with mine. It was not a partnership for *all* times, but it was a partnership for *the* times. We combined our strengths and camouflaged our weaknesses in an almost seamless process. Even after more than three decades in the business, my weaknesses are not noticeably stronger, but they are less relevant to a future that is more secure.

A Final Bow

Like all great performers, the irrepressible Mae West is deserving of an encore. Imagine Mae in an iridescent, form-fitting silver dress with one hand on a gyrating hip, cooing her famous line, "When I'm good, I'm very good, but when I'm bad, I'm better." With a pinch of literary license, that classic quote will fill the bill just fine. If Ms. West were asked to adjust her sights a bit and deliver the commencement address to the graduating class at Harvard Business School, she might just survey the sea of enraptured faces and utter in that sultry voice of hers, "If you're as good as you think you are, you're very good . . . but if you know what you're bad at, you're even better."

Masters of Their Universe

Chapter
Four

Dealing Straight

Masters of Their Universe

Secret #4

**In the long run, integrity trumps
the fleeting advantages of artifice**

Masters of Their Universe

The secret of life is honesty and fair dealing.
If you can fake that, you've got it made.

—Groucho Marx,
American actor and comedian

IN THE INVESTMENT BUSINESS, WE BLUFF,

we feign, we gyrate, we exaggerate, we dissemble. If we've been offered a bonanza price for one of our portfolio investments, we never come right out and say, "You're offering so much more than we ever hoped to receive for this company." Instead, we prompt the other side to raise its sights a bit by uttering such platitudes as, "That's certainly a respectable bid, but a bit shy of what we had in mind. We'd like you to sharpen your pencil." In another setting, we may respond to the first inquiry we receive as to the availability of one of our portfolio companies by coyly informing the potential suitor, "There's been an awful lot of interest expressed lately in ABC Healthcare, but we're certainly willing to listen to what you have to say."

In the world of commerce, we tend to employ a lexicon that translates the absolute, unvarnished truth into a dialect that bears a decent resemblance to the King's English but embellishes a bit around the edges. We often take a few liberties with the precise facts, hopefully without crossing the line into the shadowy realm of outright deceit. It's a bit like professional wrestling—while we all know that pro wrestling is not totally legit, it nevertheless is a form of entertainment that subjects the combatants to rigorous conditioning while demanding a willingness to endure pain and injury in pursuit of their career goals. The bodies may be bloated by steroids and the script written in advance, but the sweat and often the blood are real. As with the jargon used in business, we excuse the slight deviation from fidelity since we all know it's a bit of theater.

A Contest Where Nothing Is Rigged

In the wild, there is a pervasive theme of straight dealing. Inside a realm where life-and-death dramas play out without intermission, the planks of the stage are level—the predatory skills of the hunter are fairly balanced against the herd instincts and fleetness of foot of the hunted. Between predator and prey, there is a very straightforward assessment of the skills of the other, for that is what guides the endless cycle of *attack* and *escape*.

In the confrontations that do unfold, there are certainly elements of craftiness and cunning. In stalking their prey, lions crouch down so that the tufts of hair on their manes blend in with the swaying stalks of savannah grassland, and leopards use their rosette-patterned hides as camouflage to disappear within the dappled light of a grove of marula trees. I've even photographed a spotted hyena wade into the middle of a large pond, dunk its head underwater, and emerge with its jaws clenched around a bone the size of a barbell. For the hyena, the pond was the equivalent of a leopard's tree cache, a place to hide a future meal, safe from the prying eyes and flared nostrils of other predators.

To be sure, the antics of the crouching lion, the camouflaged leopard, and the wading hyena are clever ruses, but they are still well within the bounds of fair play. All the chicanery was written into the script from the outset—it is an integral part of keeping the contest evenly balanced. This drama has all the tension and tragedy and triumph of an award-winning Broadway production, but it is something more. For the audiences that are privileged to take in a performance, there is an exquisite sense of appreciation in knowing that the protagonists out there are playing for keeps . . . and thus that some of the actors will be conspicuously absent when the curtain descends.

When We Are at Our Best

There is another world where authenticity prevails and its counterpart has no place. We need no passport or plane tickets to enter that world. It is within walking distance, just a few steps away from our computers and cell phones and iPads. It is as close as our backyard, where the wildest creatures may be squirrels, and our four-legged companions have names and collars and leashes.

One of the main reasons I love our clan members the way I do—no different from millions of pet owners everywhere—is the sense of honesty and raw simplicity inherent in the relationship with a dog. The bond between men and women and their dogs has often been described as *unconditional*, and indeed there are virtually no conditions attached to the emotional ties that flow through the leash that connects the two of you.

But it is also *uncomplicated*. It is a very straightforward, simple, and honest form of love; neither side engages in fraud or deceit in order to stay attached to the other. It does not, as with most marriages and other family bonds, go through stages with sharp-elbowed curves or periods of "growing apart" and later needing to reunite. And unlike human relationships, it does not ratchet up or scale down based on changes in the master's net worth or physical beauty. In this world, we need no playbill to understand the performances, for there are no actors or costumes or scripted lines.

In many ways, we are at our very best in our relationships with our pets—generous and fair in our dealings and only too willing to extend a supportive hand to a creature that depends on us for its very existence, without expecting equal measure in return. It is a bond that is not infected with ulterior motives or sleight of hand. No wonder we walk away so devastated when that bond is cut short by the inescapable fact that our pet's DNA is calibrated to usher in its exit well before our own.

Whether I simply stroke the coat of one of our clan members or use sophisticated cameras to capture snippets of the African drama, the themes of honesty and authenticity permeate my presence in a world where deceit provides no edge to the simple thrill of being there. I never walk away feeling cheated or deceived. I only yearn to linger a bit longer in a zone—personal or geographic—where life is uncomplicated and the action is not rigged.

The Bond in a Simple Handshake

As business negotiators, we must advocate our cause with passionate zeal, but we are expected to honor the line that separates persuasive oratory from a tawdry version of fiction. For all the bluster and histrionics that spice up a tough negotiation, eventually you either walk away or you reach across the table to shake hands. And it's at the very moment when a deal is struck—when you clasp another man's or woman's hand in yours to signify that agreement has been reached—that honor and integrity must take center stage and the crafty jargon and colorful costumes of actors must be stored in a trunk, awaiting a future engagement.

Known to have been in vogue in ancient Greece at least as far back as the fifth century BC, the handshake is believed by some to have been introduced to more modern civilization in the sixteenth century by none other than Sir Walter Raleigh. Almost universally recognized today as a gesture of greeting and goodwill, the handshake is thought by many scholars to have originated as a means of demonstrating to the other person that you had no weapons in your grasp, and it was safe to engage in more civil discourse. In business, once a negotiation is concluded, the handshake signals that the dance of play-acting and jockeying for position is over. The gold standard for integrity in business can be summed up with a simple yes or no to the question, "Are you as good as your handshake?"

In the long run, dealing straight in business is not a sacrifice but rather the savvy practice of building an invaluable asset one brick at a time. There is a tendency to think of the long run and the short run as two radically different dimensions in time. But the long run has been described as nothing more than a bunch of short runs strung together. Early on in our careers, as we encounter our first few "short run" opportunities to compromise the edges of fair dealing, the temptation arises to gain a momentary advantage by drawing those edges with a blunt wandering pencil rather than a sharp razor. If that temptation did not exist in the first place, no one would ever stray from the straight and narrow. Only with the benefit of a few decades of hindsight does it become abundantly clear that each such episode is a test of our ability to add either a brick or a chink in the wall of our reputation for integrity. And like all human beings, we never post a perfect record, but hopefully we tack on more bricks than chinks.

Dealings with an LBO Potentate

I owe a substantial portion of my winnings in the field of private equity not to contortionist financial engineering or a discerning eye for the most undervalued bargains in the marketplace or even a sixth sense in terms of knowing when to exit. Instead, I attribute a great deal of my good fortune to the fact that another player in the industry—one of the giants of the trade—believed that our firm could be trusted to honor its handshake.

In 1985 with less than two years of vintage to our boutique buyout firm's history, we entered the bidding fray to become the purchaser of the flagship Dr Pepper Bottling Group of North Texas, the largest distributor of Dr Pepper in the country and part of the soft drink group controlled by LBO potentate Forstmann Little & Company. In alliance with the senior management of the bottling group, our final offer ultimately received the nod over other, more prominent groups that had considerably greater financial resources at their disposal. And thus began our firm's brief but well-documented march down the path of assembling the third largest soft drink conglomerate in US history.

As coveted as the Dr Pepper Bottling Group may have been, though, it was still not the "crown jewel" of the Dr Pepper family of companies. That sacred position belonged to the *parent* Dr Pepper Company, which manufactures the secret flavor ingredient that goes into every can and bottle of Dr Pepper. The flavor ingredient is produced by the parent company in packages of syrup or concentrate, which are then sold to soft drink bottlers all over the United States, each one dedicated to a specific geographic region. The flavoring is just one of the ingredients that the bottler adds to the brew that is poured into every container of Dr Pepper (much like the scent essence of a perfume). Without that flavor ingredient, the bottlers could not produce a single six-pack of Dr Pepper.

In 1986, just one year after our acquisition of the Texas bottling operations of Dr Pepper, Forstmann Little decided to put the parent Dr Pepper Company on the auction block. Although our firm competed for the prize, we (along with all other bidders) were left in the dust by a preemptively high offer from Coca-Cola. Though disappointed at the outcome, we could hardly be expected to best a bid by one of the largest consumer product companies in the world. Before closing the deal, however, Coke needed to secure antitrust clearance from the Federal Trade Commission (FTC). It was a final hurdle that industry observers thought would be a mere formality, particularly given that Pepsi was awaiting similar clearance for its near simultaneous purchase of 7-Up from cigarette kingpin Philip Morris. The government was not expected to block either transaction, since Coke and Pepsi were already the two gorillas in the soft drink jungle, together commanding almost a 70 percent market share of an industry that had long been dominated by the two rivals.

The consumer products world was soon rocked by a pronouncement from the FTC that it would not permit either transaction to move forward. What was thought to have been just a perfunctory approval turned into a stunning setback for Coke and Pepsi . . . and for Forstmann Little as well, whose plans to sell Dr Pepper to Coke for a knockout price had been scuttled by the FTC. As fate would have it, the two senior partners of Hicks & Haas were in contact with Goldman Sachs (Forstmann Little's investment banker) within hours after the FTC decision came down, giving our firm a chance to raise its hand before any other bidders and express our willingness to step into Coke's shoes.

In the abbreviated bidding that ensued, we emerged victorious. Like many competitive sale processes for highly valued companies, the final bids for Dr Pepper may well have been virtually indistinguishable from one another in raw dollars, but we were clearly aided by the fact that we had recently closed another major deal with Forstmann Little (the Dr Pepper bottling transaction one year earlier) without any disruption between handshake and closing; unlike a horse race, when it's a photo finish in this derby, the credibility of a bidder often earns the judge's nod.

Once we were advised by Goldman Sachs that we had been selected by Forstmann Little to purchase the much cherished Dr Pepper Company, we did not flinch in reaching across the table to shake hands with one of the legendary juggernauts of Wall Street. Within a few weeks, that handshake had ripened into a binding purchase agreement, and we became the proud owners of Dr Pepper.

With Dr Pepper as the linchpin of our investment firm's portfolio, we immediately turned our sights to 7-Up, which was back in the hands of Philip Morris after having been cut loose from Pepsi's grasp by the same FTC ruling that freed Dr Pepper from Coke's clutches. Boosted by the strategic advantage of using Dr Pepper as a platform for integrating another large soft drink concern, we emerged as the winning bidder in the reconstructed auction for 7-Up, and soon the 7-Up brand was situated right beside Dr Pepper at the pinnacle of our portfolio.

Within the span of just a few months, we had completed the process of assembling the third largest soft drink conglomerate in US history and, in the process, had launched our firm squarely onto the national stage of private equity deal makers. And it all traced its roots to a pair of handshakes over the two Dr Pepper deals (the bottling group and the parent Dr Pepper Company), between opposing investment firms that trusted each other to honor their commitments in the helter-skelter mayhem of the buyout world.

That series of soft drink acquisitions alone would surely have been enough to slake the thirst of almost any small buyout shop in the industry. But the saga continued in a bizarre sequence of events that gave new meaning to the term *déjà vu*. In 1987, Forstmann Little decided to offer for sale another blue chip company from within its portfolio, a healthcare conglomerate by the name of Sybron. Once again, Forstmann hired Goldman Sachs to conduct a heated auction for the property, and a highly renowned European group emerged as the victor. In an uncanny repetition of the events surrounding Coke's disgorgement of its claim to Dr Pepper, the Europeans backed out of the Sybron deal at the last minute, leaving Forstmann with another broken auction. We soon received a call from representatives of Forstmann Little, offering to forgo any resumption of the auction process if we would agree to acquire Sybron at exactly the same price as the European group had balked at, "not a penny more, not a penny less." If you can imagine thrusting your hand through a telephone in Dallas and the fingers coming out the other side in New York, that's what ensued. We had another handshake with the very same titan of Wall Street from whom we had acquired Dr Pepper—once again, in the immediate aftermath of a broken auction.

This time, however, we did not waltz into the closing without incident. Our dance routine was rudely interrupted by the great stock market crash of October 19, 1987 (the date scheduled for our Sybron closing), with the Dow Jones Industrial Average plummeting 23 percent in a single day. The pin-striped bankers on Wall Street were in full-fledged panic, and our financial backers for the Sybron deal were nowhere to be found. Lawyers on all sides of the deal were hurling threats across the conference room table, but the seasoned pros at Forstmann Little remained relatively cool and calm—as did we—until a brief market rally in the immediate aftermath of the crash convinced our financing sources that perhaps Western civilization as we knew it had not come to an end after all.

With order restored—momentarily, at least— the money was pushed from our side of the table to the

Forstmann Little side, and ownership of Sybron came back the other way. At the end of a harrowing week, we reached across the table, once again, to shake hands with Teddy Forstmann, Nick Forstmann, and Brian Little, three legendary figures in LBO history. When our hands clasped, there was a mutual recognition that our trust in each other had helped salvage the day in the midst of the pandemonium that reigned supreme on the streets of Gotham. As in the case of Dr Pepper, Forstmann Little cashed in another winner from its portfolio, and we saddled up on a steed named Sybron that would eventually join Dr Pepper/7-Up as the most valuable thoroughbreds in our stable of companies.

A series of handshakes just two years apart sealed more than just a few acquisitions. Those deals sealed our national reputation in the private equity world as well as our personal financial futures. There is a profound measure of nostalgia in looking back at events that transpired a quarter century ago, knowing that our firm's reputation for straight dealing played a key role in garnering those prized acquisitions.

Never Tamper with Mother Nature

Fair fights in the African bush are usually just that: fair. But not all confrontations jibe with our notion of fairness. Some seem more deserving of the labels _cruel_ and _savage_ and _heartless_. One afternoon in the Sabi Sand Reserve of South Africa, our jeep stumbled across just such a scene. A large herd of buffalos, normally docile, lumbering beasts, were in a state of frenzy, snorting and stomping around, clearly searching for something in the surrounding bush. When we spotted a dead lion cub lying in the clearing, we figured that the trio of cubs we had come across the day before had somehow managed to wander away from the safety of their nearby lair, probably when the adults were off hunting. At that point, the buffalos instinctively clicked into search-and-destroy mode, even though the cubs were only a miniature version of their deadly foe.

A second cub was nowhere to be found (presumably having escaped back to the lair), but the third was crouched under a small bush—trembling, breathing hard, and perhaps critically wounded. With the buffalos still incensed by the lion aroma in the air, we waited helplessly for the eventual discovery and mauling to unfold. But it never did. After what seemed like hours, the buffalos gave up the search and wandered off.

Darkness was about to descend, and we were torn between somehow trying to capture the cub to save its life and the proscription that you never intervene in the wild, you only observe. Long-standing tradition holds that it is not a human world, and it is not our place to influence the outcome of life-and-death struggles. Reluctantly, we retreated to camp, convinced that the cub would not last the night.

In the morning, we decided to head over to the lion's den where the adults would presumably be tending to the one cub that had escaped. What we found was the second cub as well, still breathing heavily and somewhat battered physically, but nevertheless alive and at its mother's side.

We'll never know how that cub found its way back to the den—whether on its own guided by instinct or gently carried in the jaws of its mother after she found it later that night. Nor will we ever know for sure whether the cub recovered from its wounds. But what we do know is that we had honored the integrity of the wild by not intervening. Even though we had done nothing—or perhaps precisely *because* we had done nothing—we drove away from that panting cub and its fiercely protective mother with an even greater appreciation for a realm where authenticity reigns and deceit has no currency.

Masters of Their Universe

Chapter Five

The Eyes Have It

Masters of Their Universe

Secret #5

*Your eyes are the most potent weapon
in your arsenal*

Masters of Their Universe

It is necessary to keep one's compass in one's eyes
and not in the hand, for the hands execute, but the eye judges.

—Michelangelo,
Renaissance sculptor, painter, architect, and poet

NEGOTIATING A COMPLEX BUSINESS DEAL

is not a binary process in which whatever I win, you lose. Rather, it's a Rubik's Cube of twisting and turning and retwisting and re-turning, where at the end of the day, the colors are rarely arranged in perfect alignment. While each side is armed with its charts and graphs, and computers spit out an endless stream of numbers, the negotiation itself is a more nuanced dance. And in that dance, you depend not on physical prowess but on your senses to choreograph your next move.

Bookstore shelves are stocked full of manuals purporting to unlock the mysteries of how to negotiate. But the countless bibles on the art of negotiation rarely focus on the *visual* interplay between opposing parties. Regardless of the number of legs on which it stands, a creature's vision is both a beacon that emits signals and a vessel that receives input and passes its messages on to the brain. In a conference room and in the animal kingdom, the inbound and outbound functions of the eyes are constantly at work.

With a more limited array of vocalizations at their disposal, animals depend more on visual cues to communicate—an eyeball-to-eyeball engagement to signal that aggression is called for, or a glancing away to indicate that it is not. There is much to be learned from those four-legged professors by ratcheting up our dependence on our eyes to unearth the secrets to many a riddle in the two-legged world.

The Notion of "Cerebral Vision"

When I give graduate school lectures, I am often quizzed about the relationship between my twin professions of business and photography, strange bedfellows indeed. One question that frequently arises is, "Which specific trait from your investment career was most valuable to you as a photographer, and vice versa?" In those somewhat formal classroom settings, I usually respond by focusing on the value of being a perfectionist or displaying perseverance in the face of adversity. But the trait that matters most in both callings is something else entirely: *my eyesight.*

It's not so much eyesight in the sense that an optometrist would measure your ocular prowess as 20/20. Instead, it is the more cerebral ability to convert ordinary "looking around" into an intense focus that pierces through each layer of impressions much as one would dissect an artichoke to reach its core. The eyes act as a periscope to scan the horizon and communicate their findings to the brain, which in turn digests the data and arrives at a steady stream of decisions. During such episodes of intense visual concentration, the brain adheres to the principle that you rarely learn anything when your mouth is moving.

Neither my eyesight nor my hearing is terribly acute, but that is of little consequence. For it isn't the acuity of my vision that I count on most heavily as an investor or an artist. It is eyesight in the sense of visual concentration rather than microscopic detection—something akin to *cerebral vision.*

Years ago, in the midst of a sweltering afternoon in southern Africa, I attempted to capture freeze-frame shots of a pair of lilac-breasted rollers—an uncanny creature of airborne exotica that appears to have been doused by all the colors on an artist's palette and yet somehow arranged the hues in a perfectly symmetrical mosaic of turquoise, pink, green, beige, orange, scarlet, and sapphire. At rest, it is a sight to behold; in flight, it is a grail to be captured.

On this particular afternoon, when the sun blistered the earth to the point that mammals sought the shelter of shaded groves, a pair of lilac-breasted rollers flitted only a few feet off the ground, departing from and returning to the same downed log whose branches lifted skyward like outstretched arms. I parked myself behind another felled tree about thirty feet away and crouched down so as not to be visible to the skittish birds. And I just watched, trying to figure out how to capture images that would freeze the body and extended wingspan of that aerial palette.

The birds may have been moving at a speed that defied my ability to rotate my lens in sync with their flight patterns, but their favorite branch—the one that served as their runway—was not. So I trained my lens on that branch and tried to anticipate when one of the rollers would alight or when one that was perched would take wing. If I guessed just right, that streak of hues would find itself exactly parallel to the branch and thus perfectly in focus. I spent all afternoon lying on my belly, soaked through with sweat, clicking down incessantly on the shutter button. I rarely hit it right, but when I did, the images were as crisp as if the rollers had been plucked from midair and preserved forevermore by a taxidermist, impossibly brilliant colors in moment-freezing alignment.

In attempting to photograph those birds in flight, I was imitating the behavior of the predators that had captured my imagination from the moment I first set foot on African soil. Each one stares at its prey incessantly, plotting its line of attack and tolerating the fact that *missing* is far more likely than *hitting* in the choreography of predation.

The visual prowess of African predators is simply mind-boggling—the ability of a lion to stare into a vibrating, nearly formless pattern of black-and-white stripes that is a herd of galloping zebras and isolate the one that is slightly lame. To capture such moments on film, wildlife photographers must imitate our target—we must engage our visual concentration and zero in on the predator (the "prey" of our artistic endeavors) and anticipate its movements and the exact moment of attack.

Looking for Clues in Your Own Backyard

To witness the overarching power of eyesight in the animal realm, you needn't hop a flight to Botswana. A leisurely stroll in the local dog park or even around your own home is journey enough. The gang of mutts that roam our property sometimes seems like a troop of playful actors that reprise the deadly drama unfolding a continent away. No residue of their wolf heritage has been handed down with greater fidelity than the role of eyesight in their lives. Their other senses are certainly razor sharp as well, but none seems to count more than eyesight. As with their more feral ancestors, visual clues are constantly exchanged within the clan in an unending sequence of invitations to either dance or fight.

Even the most innocent of sightings by one of our clan members sometimes arouses a more serious instinct— as when the young cockapoo, Cooper, is the first to spot a suitcase that normally accompanies his human parents on a trip somewhere. The slightest glimpse of that suitcase will trigger a spasm of nervousness that immediately spreads to the other members of the clan as the fear of abandonment settles in. Not until each one is leashed and we are on our way to the airport en masse will calm be restored.

The predatory use of sight on which their ancestors depended for survival is evident on those few occasions when one of the guys eyeballs a squirrel that has placed itself in harm's way, too far from the safe haven of a tree to avoid capture by a clan member that lowers its head before launching an attack. The clan instinctively gauges when the distance between a squirrel and the nearest tree is tempting enough to give chase, rarely expending energy in a totally hopeless effort.

On more serious occasions, the warning signs for the impending outbreak of hostilities are unmistakable. Normally a submissive creature, our largest dog, Spencer, will occasionally be goaded too far by the burgeoning alpha Henry. Provoked beyond his limits by one of Henry's aggressive glares, an almost otherworldly transformation overtakes Spencer's eyes that foreshadows all-out war unless his fit is intercepted. His eyelids descend to half-mast as Spencer takes the measure of Henry eyeball-to-eyeball, and one would swear that the color of his hooded eyes has visibly darkened. Spencer has entered another zone altogether, and a different animal has taken control of his psyche. In the binary decision tree of fight or flight, Spencer has made his choice. Unless I am there to massage his ears and whisper soothing words, Spencer is on autopilot for an attack. Henry has learned to recognize Spencer's transformation and usually opts to fight another day, diverting his gaze and breaking the visual deadlock.

The most basic instincts within our collection of mutts—fear of abandonment, hunting, and intramural aggression—each depend on visual prowess and the signals that originate from those very same eyes. At such moments, the members of the clan have much in common with their wild brethren in Africa—and their behavior is a sight to behold.

Making—and Avoiding—Eye Contact

Regrettably, with the viral spread of e-mail, fewer episodes of negotiation are conducted face-to-face anymore, let alone in the chambers of an elegant conference room with upholstered antique chairs and a mahogany table that seems to stretch from one zip code to another. The dramatic interludes of in-person fencing among suited swordsmen with crisp white shirts and Windsor-knotted ties have often given way to conference calls among players attired in jeans or even the tone-deaf medium of e-mail.

But rare is the deal that proceeds from opening to closing without any face-to-face meetings. Though few in number, the in-person sessions are of utmost importance, for it is in those meetings when you take the measure of your opponent, and your opponent of you. The face-to-face impressions inform all the subsequent negotiating sessions—even the ones conducted by conference call or through proxies such as lawyers.

Too often, the art of negotiation is described in terms that portray the "winner" as the party that overwhelms its opponent by slinging gallons of testosterone across the conference room table in a display of raw, unbridled power. Instead, I favor a more direct, less threatening approach, often asking my counterpart at the outset, "What are your objectives? What are you trying to achieve with this deal?" And then I watch. At that point, it's time to engage the power of eyesight and observe the subtle shifts in facial expression and body language as each goal is described by the other side, detecting when visual clues betray the bravado of a bluffer as opposed to the sincerity of a true advocate. Sometimes highly charged phrases such as "deal-breaker" are uttered simply to bully and at other times with genuine feeling—and your eyes are your best tool for interpreting the true meaning. By concentrating on the opposing party's mannerisms, we are usually able to detect the difference between the empty histrionics of arm-waving and the resolve that underpins a firm position. In the words of the Greek philosopher Heraclitus, "The eyes are more exact witnesses than the ears."

Even when you're in the process of delivering a soliloquy that you feel must surely be the equal of Hamlet's "To be or not to be . . . ," there is much to be gained by keeping your eyes fixed on the members of the opposing team. By doing so, you are better able to decipher the impact—both positive and negative—of your oratorical efforts. Your adversaries will not be equally enraptured with every syllable you utter, and visual focus will reveal clues as to where your bargaining fortress needs to be buttressed and where it is secure.

At its best, eye contact will create a connection, a common ground for effective discourse and reasoned compromise. But at the other extreme, the opposing parties in a business duel may glare at each other eyeball-to-eyeball until one literally blinks—and a great deal of trust can be lost in that blink of an eye.

In a merger negotiation a few years ago, I detected a distinct skittishness in the two lead principals on the other side whenever I would forcefully address a point of contention, noting a failure on their part to maintain eye contact with me for more than a few seconds at a time. There is an intimacy and a power to eye contact that is palpable in face-to-face negotiations. In this case, it was abundantly clear that maintaining eye contact with me was simply uncomfortable for the two negotiators on the other side. At first that seemed odd, since on a number of prior occasions we had worked together as cohorts on deals and the two invariably had deferred to my lead as chief negotiator. Eventually I surmised that perhaps they now felt intimidated sitting on opposite sides of the table.

As much as we may covet the labels of being a "shrewd" or "fierce" negotiator, that reputation is sometimes more of a liability than an asset as we enter the negotiations for our next deal. It may engender in our counterpart an extreme cautiousness—a hesitancy to concede or compromise—that makes good deal making almost impossible to conduct. And maintaining eye contact with an intimidated rival may only reinforce those tendencies.

Presuming that to be the case here, I thought it best to avoid further face-to-face bargaining sessions for fear of provoking knee-jerk intransigence on the other side. The future negotiations were all conducted via conference call, as we opted to draw some distance between the parties and limit the amount of direct eye contact. With this shift in approach, I was able to access each of my two counterparts in one-on-one or two-on-one telephone chats. This proved conducive to restoring a more congenial atmosphere, and we managed to weave our way through an intricate web of issues that seemed more daunting when we were meeting in person. In the process, we afforded our eyes a welcome sabbatical.

In the animal world—both wild and domesticated—eye contact between rivals will often inflame the level of hostility until either fisticuffs erupt or one of the adversaries chooses to divert its gaze. This negotiating episode offered up a clear illustration of how the eyes are an incredibly potent instrument in a bargaining session, capable of either bridging a gulf or driving a deeper wedge between the parties.

The Eyes of the Elephant
In focusing on the parallels between the role of eyesight in animal behavior and in the tricky waters of a complex negotiation, it is worth noting that no facial feature of humans and four-legged creatures resemble each other as much as the eyes do. We each use our eyes in a similar two-directional way—to decipher what we absorb from the world around us and to emit signals that reveal our innermost thoughts and emotions.

To my way of thinking, there is no better place than Africa to master the art of interpreting visual interplay. As a wildlife photographer, I learned early on to study my subjects' eyes for clues as to what their next move would be or when I had ventured too close and encroached on the "no-fly zone" that must be maintained to avoid placing myself at risk. There is no precise way to gauge the width of that zone—it shrinks or expands depending on the presence of young in the vicinity, whether a fresh carcass needs to be protected, and for other reasons known only to your subject. The best you can do is just stare in their eyes and try to fathom the unfathomable.

But not all creatures' eyes emit signals that are equally well understood by humans. Some are more inscrutable than others, and sometimes my imagination—percolating in the harsh African sun—would conjure up things that were probably never there.

Staring into a lion's amber eyes or the orange glow of a cheetah's, I never knew for sure what was passing through that recessed feline mind. The language of their thoughts was not the language of my own. We communicated only in the tongue of fight or flight.

But when my eyes made contact with those on an elephant's massive skull, I felt a twinge that our minds made contact too. Never for a moment did I see myself as a higher being in this communion—we were equals, just packaged differently. Behind those shrouded eyes, the elephant knew full well that my species was to be trusted not at all. Though my hands gripped nothing more lethal than a camera, my brethren had visited the worst upon its kin, bartering tusks for princely gain, leaving rotting flesh and orphaned calves behind. I felt the power of their melancholy. Inside myself, I felt the searing burn of shame.

The bonds of trust were broken long ago. I sensed that most acutely among the eldest of the herd, the ones whose sunken temples have that look of age. And as we parted ways, I thought back to more distant times when our ancestors would go their separate ways in peace, exchanging admiring glances back and forth.

Masters of Their Universe

Chapter Six

Barbarians at the Gate

Masters of Their Universe

Secret #6

*Know the limits of your own territory—
perhaps the world is flat after all*

Masters of Their Universe

The only reason some people get lost in thought
is because it's unfamiliar territory.

—Paul Fix,
American actor and town marshal in
the TV Western *The Rifleman*

CONJURING UP AN IMAGE OF A CIVILIZED
people defending their fortress against a horde of philistines,
Barbarians at the Gate is the apt title of a book by Bryan
Burrough and John Helyar that recounts the 1988 wrestling
match between kingpins of the leveraged buyout industry over
the acquisition of consumer giant RJR Nabisco. Ultimately,
the titans of finance and their armies of advisors were swept
up in a whirlpool of greed, ego, and swashbuckling tactics that
left observers stunned at the lengths to which the characters
would go to seize control of a juicy corporate target.

In the final analysis, *Barbarians* is all about territory
and the wisdom of knowing your own limits—sensing when
to defend your turf against unwelcome intruders, and how
to recognize when greed and hubris have tempted you to
wander far outside the borders of reasoned judgment. It is
a stark reminder that the so-called masters of the universe
in the investment business must not take that moniker
too seriously, for the limits of their prowess are far more
circumscribed than that bloated label would imply.

Defining What Is Yours to Defend

The dual lessons of defining what is yours to defend and respecting the borders that you must not transgress have no better professors than the four-legged ones that roam the African wilderness and the more docile ones that curl up on your lap at night.

The seriousness of exercising territorial dominion is abundantly clear in the ferocious barking that a canine clan displays all along the edge of a fence that marks the boundary of its home turf. Joggers, walkers, deliverymen, other dogs, and sometimes even passing cars are treated with equal measures of disdain and aggression. If any of those potential interlopers approaches the front gates directly, the intensity of canine hostility ratchets up a notch or two. Even dogs that have never experienced a break-in or other perimeter breach react as if their very source of livelihood were at stake.

Somewhat more amusing from our point of view—but undoubtedly just as serious from theirs—is the practiced minuet of territorial markings. In the case of our clan, each of the guys seems to have his own particular collection of trees, bushes, and fence posts that merits a squirt or two on virtually every outing. Several landmarks are particularly choice locations, earning double or even triple markings from a sequence of two or three clan members (as if to say, "This is our sacred turf . . . and we're not kidding, buddy!"). Even a casual inspection of our property will reveal where the guys have firmly planted their flag in the ground—it's where the foliage has noticeably yellowed and withered over the years in the face of an unrelenting urinary assault.

A canine clan that decorates its property with pungent markings may do so with solemn intent, as if it were a matter of life and death. But in the African theater, the boundary of a predator's territory is no laughing matter—out there, it often *is* a matter of life and death. In its ultimate wisdom, the grand architect of the African plains did not erect natural fences to divvy up the landscape into a checkerboard pattern allocated among the inhabitants. Seasonal weather fluctuations have forced prey herds to roam in search of water, and predators are left with no choice other than to roam along with the herds or carve up the land into fiefdoms as if to declare, "Whoever happens to graze or hunt within my little piece of the universe is mine to devour or attack. Enter at your own risk!"

With urinary and fecal markings whose odors are unmistakable to creatures imbued with a sense of smell many times more powerful than our own, African predators know full well the limits of their own turf and the entry point to someone else's. Out there, it is crucial to defend your own territory against invasion, but equally important not to wander into unfamiliar zones controlled by others.

Half a globe away from the African savannah, I once photographed from the air a contingent of brown bears chasing salmon in the tidal flats of Iniskin Bay, Alaska. Each bear would position itself at its own strategic spot in the shallow waters of the bay as thousands of salmon wriggled past. Even though there was plenty of salmon for all to devour, if one of the bears wandered into the ill-defined—to my eyes at least—turf of another, the irate bear would give chase to the intruder to the "delight" of the salmon that would just mosey on by. Each bear somehow knew how to define the limits of the tidal flats over which it reigned supreme and the perils of crossing over into the watery province of another.

Our Little Corner in the Neighborhood

Although the private equity world has not degenerated (yet) to the point where we "masters of the universe" resort to urinary streams to mark our turf, it is nevertheless a highly competitive landscape where territorial rights still play a pivotal role. However, the most deadly peril that practitioners of the trade encounter is not the one inherent in protecting our turf against a competitor's entry, but rather the risk of failing to recognize the hazards of wandering outside the bounds of familiar territory.

The coordinates that define your position on the field of private equity are multiple, including such variables as the industries in which you specialize, the geographic regions where you choose to invest, the number of office locations and investment professionals in your operation, and the aggregate amount of capital at your command. As on a baseball diamond, the essence of a well-crafted strategy is one in which each variable is assigned a right-field line and a left-field line that define the field of play—and beyond those chalk-filled markers, you run the risk of crossing over into foul territory.

Buyout artists must develop a prodigious capacity for being quick studies—the frenetic pace of our trade sometimes requires that we immerse ourselves in the inner workings of an industry and a specific target company within a matter of a few months (or even weeks) before reaching an investment decision.

In contrast with some of my brethren in the industry, I always felt most comfortable in this fast-paced world adhering to a very simple game plan within the confines of a relatively small firm. I found the business to be treacherous enough without constantly adjusting upward the scope of our operations or the range of our investment activities. We executed our strategy with almost mind-numbing consistency and with strict regard for the territorial limits we had set. For more than twenty-five years, our firm operated under one roof in Dallas, with five or fewer partners, focused primarily on consumer products and healthcare, making no investments outside North America, having less than ten portfolio companies at any one time, and concentrating on smaller "middle market" deals rather than the multibillion-dollar acquisitions pursued by jumbo funds.

Exotic and unpredictable we were not. While the private equity world around us multiplied one hundred times in size, extending its tentacles to emerging markets around the world and into the nooks and crannies of arcane industries, we basically kept our eyes fixed on those left-field and right-field lines, figuring that there was sufficient reward (and plenty of risk) in our own bailiwick without trespassing on unfamiliar turf. In the perilous landscape of private equity, we stumbled often enough on the obstacles that lay within our own territory, emerging with slimmer pocketbooks and bruised egos. Early on, I concluded that the best way to smooth out the wrinkles in the roller coaster of our business was to simplify the journey so that it resembled a straightforward train ride to a well-known destination—I figured that it's hard to get lost on the train.

One reason I found *Barbarians at the Gate* so fascinating was the precise timing of when that saga unfolded. When the book was first published in 1990, we had already brought to a glorious and rewarding finale the implausible string of good fortune that had rained down on our small buyout firm Hicks & Haas. Within the span of just six years, we had found the cashier's window for our most celebrated acquisitions, deciding that to linger any longer would have been tempting fate. We figured it was time to divvy up the spoils before the fairy dust turned to sawdust.

In that sense, we appreciated the most critical territorial limit of all in the gerrymandered realm of private equity—the constantly shifting and exceedingly thin line that separates fortuitous gain from disastrous loss. That line is a dynamic one that shifts dramatically and without warning. Shortly after we had engineered our portfolio's hurried exit from the stage, the fickle market for junk bonds—which provided the underlying octane for such bloated prices as the RJR Nabisco buyout—collapsed in a heap, dragging down values in the volatile LBO sector. Recognizing when *enough is enough* and having the discipline to cash in your chips before the odds turn against you is a priceless lesson in territorial limits.

After cashing out in 1989, I opted to salt away the lion's share of the bounty that we had unearthed and just watch from a distance for several years, more out of fear of the unknown than any more lofty instinct. Once I did venture out again, I chose to gamble less, now that I had something meaningful to lose.

Of Bubbles and Ducklings
In 1999, I delivered a lecture at the Yale School of Management during the heyday of the dot-com bubble when barely hatched technology ducklings were trading with values in the hundreds of millions of dollars, even though

their first glimmers of profitability were not yet visible. At the end of my lecture, virtually every follow-up question from the students related to technology start-ups, about which I knew next to nothing except that the valuations seemed to be outrageous—and I said so. I must have seemed like an aging dinosaur on the verge of extinction.

In retrospect, I was not a gifted soothsayer of the doom that ultimately awaited most dot-com investments. I was just exceedingly skeptical of the "new paradigm" that was in vogue as to the value of companies that I thought still belonged in an incubator. What I did recognize was the fact that I didn't know enough about those high-tech sectors to wander off our more parochial but familiar turf. Eventually, our restraint proved to be the more prudent course, as the *new paradigm* deteriorated into a mere *pair of dimes*. And the practitioners of our trade were served up with a bitter—or gratifying—reminder of the well-known children's fable in which the plodding tortoise prevails in its race against the speedy hare.

I have always subscribed to an unwritten rule that our investment firm shouldn't pursue any deal if I don't understand what the company in question does for a living. That has the distinct advantage of limiting our periscope of investigation to an incredibly small number of companies. Having survived for three decades in a business in which roadkill is scattered all over the highway, we have become even more selective and conservative than ever. Like the predators in the African savannah that know the boundaries of their small piece of the universe and resist the temptation to cross over into a competitor's turf, we have learned the value of respecting territorial limits and found that our best deals are often the ones we choose not to do.

Masters of Their Universe

Chapter Seven

Power Plays

Masters of Their Universe

Secret #7

*In a negotiation,
you have as much leverage
as the other side thinks you have*

Masters of Their Universe

Never appeal to a man's "better nature." ...
Invoking his self-interest gives you more leverage.

—Lazarus Long,
fictional character in novels by Robert A. Heinlein

ENDOWED BY HIS CREATOR HEINLEIN WITH

the ability to live for hundreds of years through the aid of rejuvenation treatments, wise old Lazarus does not leave us dangling quite as much as Yogi Berra did with his guidance to "take it" whenever we come to a fork in the road. In a single sentence ("Invoking his self-interest gives you more leverage"), Lazarus lays bare two cornerstones of effective negotiating that I've witnessed over the past few decades: (1) there are distinct advantages to focusing on your counterpart's self-interest as opposed to just your own and (2) the leverage in a negotiation is not an absolute, immutable force, but something more malleable that you may shape to your advantage.

There is a widespread tendency to view the leverage at work in a business duel much as you would a tug-of-war at opposite ends of a rope. A tug-of-war is a zero sum game: whenever I manage to pull you forward toward the centerline, I can move back an equal distance, and vice versa. It is simply a contest of brute force with virtually no finesse at all.

But tug-of-war is not a particularly good analogy to the art of negotiating, nor is it very useful in deciphering how leverage works in fashioning a business deal. The use of leverage is much more akin to boxing or karate, where your sensitivity to an opponent's lunges and maneuvers—and his or her appreciation for yours—are the keys to success. It sometimes is more psychological in nature than it is a contest of raw power. Particularly when you find yourself in a vulnerable position, you can be a much more effective negotiator if you subscribe to the belief that the amount of leverage at your disposal is not a fixed commodity, but rather is equal to whatever your adversary believes you to possess.

The One Who Would Be King
In the wild and among a troop of canines in your own backyard, there is one negotiation, in particular, that repeats itself over and over during the lifetimes of the clan members. That negotiation centers on the ultimate question of pack life: *who is the leader of this clan?*

In the savannah grasslands of Africa, clan leadership is often the most demanding and dangerous role of all. Whenever there is a challenge to the hegemony of a male who heads a lion pride, it is the leader whose life is at stake when a younger, stronger male challenges an aging master. In the physical confrontation that ensues between the one who sits atop the throne and the challenger who would be king, the other members of the pride are perfectly content to be mere spectators at what is invariably a savage contest, watching with rapt attention but without any apparent favorite. Once the confrontation is over, if the old leader lies dead or grievously wounded, the followers simply change T-shirts from his brand to the upstart's.

After one such bloody encounter, I watched in silence as a pair of young turks who had mounted a challenge to the reigning pride leader limped away in defeat, with open chest wounds staining their tawny hides in red. The battle had also taken a visible toll on the victor, who was then most vulnerable to another's challenge. But there was an aura of invincibility that cloaked his every move—no other males in the vicinity opted to engage in battle with this head of pride. The fresh image of his having knocked off two pretenders to the throne was apparently all the leverage this battle-scarred veteran needed to dissuade others from mounting an attack on his kingship.

A Sweet Result from a Soured Deal

Over the course of my investment career, I have been involved in many negotiations in which our side of the table was clearly outgunned in terms of *objective* leverage, and the task at hand was to figure out how to knit the proverbial silk purse out of a sow's ear. One such episode unfolded when I first stumbled onto the stage of private equity back in the late 1970s. The senior partners of our venture capital firm charged me with the task of exiting from a soured investment in a company that was teetering on the brink of insolvency. The assignment was to finalize the terms of sale to a pair of industry veterans who were represented by an incredibly abrasive (and reputedly anti-Semitic) lawyer.

Spurred on at first by an instinctive reaction to the arrogance exhibited by my adversaries, I sought to frustrate their efforts to steamroll through the negotiations by asking an endless stream of questions about their objectives, their perception of ours, and how the two sets of objectives could be squared with each other. After a while, I could see that my delaying tactics were causing blood to boil and nerves to fray on the other side. The negotiations dragged on and on without any apparent end in sight.

Frustrated to the point of losing his cool, the offensive lawyer went over my head and complained to one of my senior partners that I was totally impossible to deal with and that his clients were on the verge of walking away and watching our troubled company collapse in their wake. In the course of an ensuing one-on-one fireside chat with my senior partner, I was urged to throttle back and save my daredevil tactics for a deal where we had something meaningful to gain. I resisted the notion that we should simply capitulate and suggested instead that my tactics must be on the verge of bearing fruit or else the opposing lawyer would never have complained about my stubbornness in the first place.

Impatient with my upstart antics, the senior partner blurted out, "Bobby, we don't have any leverage in this negotiation!" to which I calmly replied, "No, sir, that's not quite right. . . . We have exactly as much leverage as those bastards think we have." For a few seconds, my comment just hung in the air. Then, with a dismissive flick of the wrist and a faint smile, the partner released me on my own recognizance back into the negotiating arena.

I didn't return to the bargaining table with any more leverage in an objective sense than I had when I caucused privately with my partner. I was still saddled with a wounded company that had nowhere else to turn. But I was convinced that I could maximize our leverage not through the exercise of raw power (as to which the other side had a monopoly), but by subtly persuading our adversaries that we might well have acceptable alternatives. While my knee-jerk response to the senior partner's comment about our not having any leverage may have been uttered in a fit of bravado, it was spot on—we had exactly as much as our opponents thought we had. The other side certainly *suspected* that we had no viable options, but for all they knew, I was negotiating with them on Mondays, Wednesdays, and Fridays, and with someone else on Tuesdays and Thursdays.

At first, it was all a gambit, simply bargaining for time like a prisoner on death row knowing that the day of reckoning is coming soon. But at some point, the exercise in foiling their efforts evolved into a conscious strategy. I began to weave together a structure for the transaction that would allow the other side to achieve all its major objectives and yet still leave a few crumbs along the side of the road for us. Eventually, the crumbs added up to half a loaf, and we emerged with a very respectable deal, certainly far better than we expected when the negotiations began. I was thrilled, not only by the spoils of victory but also because that lawyer left the closing with red cheeks and spittle at the edge of his mouth after I offered my hand in mock congratulations.

Top Dog
Unlike their wild brethren, being the head of a domesticated canine troop is not associated with the privilege of exclusive mating status or the premier position at the dinner table of a fresh kill. The contest for the alpha position is a more

delicate negotiation in which the rewards are subtler and the casualties less deadly. But leadership is nevertheless a highly coveted position, even among the most pampered four-legged darlings of the Rodeo Drive set.

Simply staring at the mug shots of the members of a pack of mutts will not necessarily yield a good guess as to which one is the alpha male. In our case, that title always belonged to Oliver. When Oliver first arrived on the scene as a three-month-old rescue of suspect lineage (probably a Lhasa-poodle mix), there was no clan to lead. Everyone else in the house had just two legs, and this foundling puppy from the parking lot of an abandoned apartment building established his unchallenged position by bonding with his two human parents. Eventually, Oliver would be surrounded by four other mixed-breed males. At first, his leadership went unchallenged, but eventually Henry (four years his junior and considerably stronger) launched periodic assaults designed to unseat Oliver from the throne—but the scepter of clan leadership never changed paws.

In his later years, the passage of time robbed an aging Oliver of virtually all his sight and most of his hearing, and a paralyzing tumble down an embankment deprived him of the use of his back legs. But outfitted with a doggie chariot that allowed him to amble around on two back wheels and two front legs, Oliver kept his rear end planted firmly on the seat of power.

A while back, I was sharing a Corona with Oliver beside the small pond behind our home—my job to consume the amber liquid on the inside and his to lick the perspiring bottle on the outside. I watched Ollie stare in the direction of the pond through cataract-filled eyes, and I realized that the most confounding thing about his recovery from every imaginable assault on his body was how a nearly blind and partially paralyzed dog managed to keep his leadership intact. Henry still coveted the scepter, but Oliver offered up not the slightest hint that a new coronation ceremony was in the offing. Through the *perception* of leverage—the well-timed growl, the brief fracas, the absence of any sign of submissiveness—Oliver maintained his alpha position well into his sunset years with periodic reminders that the throne was his by right if not by might.

Pulling Those Levers in the Emerald City

Over the years, I have given many graduate school lectures on the art of negotiation, which have centered on the saga of Dr Pepper and 7-Up: How in 1986 our boutique buyout firm acquired first Dr Pepper and then 7-Up, merged the operations of the two, and then engineered one of the more lucrative exits in LBO history. That tale unfolded with all the twists and turns of a Broadway play, with the actors at center stage walking away to the thunderous sound of shekels—not flowers or applause—being tossed their way as the curtain came down at the end of a two-year run.

The underlying current that allowed our small investment firm to launch the good ship *Dr Pepper/7-Up* was the same one that propelled Hicks & Haas throughout its entire six-year tenure in the buyout business. We operated on the simple premise that in capturing and negotiating deals, *you have exactly as much leverage as the other side thinks you have.*

Almost thirty years ago, our fledgling firm entered the fray in the early days of the buyout industry much the way that Oliver spent the last few years lording over his pack of mutts—handicapped by circumstance but undaunted in our ambitious quest. Oliver had virtually no sight or hearing, and we had no pool of capital under our control. Oliver moved forward without his back legs, and we sprinted onto the scene without an illustrious track record.

All we had was a home-grown strategy for how to position ourselves at the center of gravity of each of our deals. Once we set our sights on what appeared to be an attractive buyout, we would undertake our due diligence investigation and, in the process, convince senior management of the target company that we would both be best served by locking arms with one another when we sought financing for the buyout. Once aligned with management, we jointly approached Wall Street for the required financing, carving out for ourselves a healthy slice of ownership that was wholly disproportionate to the meager amount of capital we would be investing.

With exaggerated swagger in our step, we would march right up to the bankers declaring for all the world to hear, "We have the deal in tow, we have the allegiance of senior management . . . all we need is the lion's share of the money." In today's more sophisticated and institutionalized world of finance, we would be laughed out of the offices of the firms that occupy center stage in the financial district (or tossed out one of their sixtieth-floor windows). But this was almost thirty years ago in the pioneer days of the LBO business, when brash strangers from the badlands of Texas sometimes showed up in New York wearing coonskin caps with tall tales of the fabulous riches to be earned out west.

In the course of a critical conference with one such bank group during the Dr Pepper/7-Up odyssey, there was an awkward moment that almost managed to pull back the curtain on our well-practiced imitation of the Wizard of Oz (who, after all, was just pulling levers and belching smoke). At the end of a brief presentation by the senior management of Dr Pepper, one of the heavyweights at this Wall Street firm leaned back in his chair and posed a blunt (but eminently reasonable) question: "I understand why senior management will be receiving a sizable share of the ownership if we do this deal—after all, we'll be depending on that management team to implement the operating plan. And I understand why the financiers here in New York will also be receiving a large share—we'll be providing almost 100 percent of the capital for the buyout. What I don't understand for the life of me is why Hicks & Haas will be receiving such a large chunk of ownership. It won't be either managing the company or investing more than a token amount of money."

There was heavy silence in the room as all eyes turned to the tall strangers from Texas, who appeared perilously close to being exposed. But shame on us if we hadn't been well prepared for that question, since we imagined many times before that it would eventually come up. Without missing a beat, we responded with something along the lines of, "The reason is this: Our firm brought this deal into your office, and we brought senior management in here as well. If you choose not to finance the buyout with our firm, that's fine. We'll just march right across the street and finance it with one of your competitors . . . and when we walk out that door, this troop of senior managers will follow right behind us."

In retrospect, it *was* a rather galling thing to say. Like the mustachioed Wizard in the Emerald City with his outrageous jacket and bejeweled turban, all we had in our hands were those levers. But we had created the *perception of leverage*—we were promising the Cowardly Lion courage, the Tin Man a heart, and the Scarecrow a brain. We convinced those Wall Street firms to believe in the story, to fall in line, and to walk behind us as we followed the yellow brick road. And like the Wizard, we delivered on our promises.

We Are All Just Actors

To achieve the desired result in any negotiation where the objective state of affairs tilts heavily in favor of the other side, you must be able to do a bit of role-playing. The key is to be so convincing in your portrayal of a party who has access to other viable options that even *you* aren't totally sure at the end of the day whether you're acting or not.

The Bard of Avon, William Shakespeare, understood four centuries ago that the business of life has much in common with the art of acting:

> *All the world's a stage,*
> *And all the men and women merely players,*
> *They have their exits and their entrances,*
> *And one man in his time plays many parts.*
> *—As You Like It* (Act II, Scene VII)

Our role is best fulfilled when those on the other side—be it the patrons of the Globe Theater or the players on the stage of global finance—leave their seats convinced that a fair bargain has been struck among all who entered the theater or the negotiating forum with lofty expectations as to what would unfold.

Chapter Eight

Clothes Make the Man

Masters of Their Universe

Secret #8

Don't kid yourself—appearance counts

Masters of Their Universe

Clothes make the man.
Naked people have little or no influence on society.

—Mark Twain,
American author and humorist

MARK TWAIN'S QUIP IS MOST LIKELY A

reference to one of my favorite childhood stories, aptly entitled "Clothes Make the Man" by the French author Henri Duvernois. Long after I had forgotten Duvernois's name, his short story lingered in my mind as a lesson worth tucking away in a drawer somewhere.

In the story, a trio of French thieves by the names of Tango, Mireault, and Eel plan a robbery of one of the homes in a posh district of Paris. Much to his chagrin, Tango is instructed by the gang's leader, Mireault, to don a policeman's uniform in order to divert suspicion away from the larceny that his cohorts would be committing nearby. With his barrel chest and broad shoulders, Tango is indeed an impressive sight in his new uniform. Patrolling the adjacent street while his colleagues execute their nefarious scheme, Tango grows enamored with the unfamiliar respect and authority that come his way by reason of his attire as a French gendarme—exchanging salutes with a police lieutenant, escorting an elderly lady across the street, and even seizing an abusive drunk who challenges his authority. When his two cohorts finally emerge from the home that has been pilfered, Mireault insults Tango by calling him an idiot for having taken his disguise too seriously. In an ironic twist at the end of the tale, the affronted Tango summons a cadre of police reinforcements with a shrill salvo from his whistle, shouting, "Crooks, robbers! I arrest you in the name of the law."

As a young boy, I was captivated by how a simple change of clothes could prove so pivotal. I imagined Tango living a crime-free life forever after, perhaps as one of Paris's finest.

Camouflage and Splendor in the Okavango Delta

It might seem odd that an analogy to this sartorial anecdote could be extracted from the animal world, but indeed the lesson is there for the discerning eye. In a well-known display worthy of Lady Gaga on the red carpet at the Grammy Awards, the Indian peacock spreads and quivers its ornate train of long colorful feathers in a psychedelic ritual of courtship. Hardly a frivolous gesture, studies have shown that the male's elongated plumage is actually evaluated by female peahens as a gauge of his virility when she chooses a mate from among her suitors.

While the Okavango Delta of Botswana may not boast all the ceremonial splendor of the Westminster Dog Show, it is nevertheless a place where appearance counts. As has been well documented, the earth tones and spotted hides that adorn the coats of four-legged predators allow the hunters to blend in with their surroundings and minimize the risk of detection when tracking prey. On the other hand, a male lion is well served by the exquisite length and bushiness of its classic dark mane. The longer and bushier manes are known to be preferred by females and to enjoy the added benefit of causing that enormous leonine head to appear even larger and more intimidating to rival males. In a fitting parallel to the business world, the original costume designer for African lions apparently appreciated the fact that in achieving the dual objectives of camouflage and majestic splendor, there is a delicate balance to be struck between the advantages of blending in at certain times and being a sight to behold at others.

Undoubtedly the most fascinating display I have ever witnessed of how an animal's appearance may enhance its standing among rivals is the phenomenon known as *lateral presentation*. This bizarre fighting ritual is practiced among male nyala antelopes in Africa as a choreographed form of contact-free combat.

Even standing by itself and grazing at its leisure, a male nyala is one impressive-looking creature. The male dwarfs its female counterpart with a body weight of well over two hundred pounds (roughly twice hers) on a striped torso with long spiral horns and a white dorsal crest of fur on its back. When a female comes into heat in the vicinity of two males, a surreal confrontation ensues where the adversarial bulls enter the ring of combat for mating rights with all the machismo—and none of the grievous bodily harm—of an Ali-Frazier heavyweight match.

Once the bell is sounded for the opening round, the two males move in sync around the perimeter of a tight circle, directly across from one another with heads turned to stare at their rival. With exaggerated stiffness and increasingly rigid leg movements, the opposing males elevate their hair fringe and dorsal crest in a series of moves that increase their apparent body surface by up to 40 percent. As the intensity of the drama at opposite points on the circle heightens, the movement may actually stop . . . until one of the two bulls "blinks" at how impressive and intimidating the other's appearance has become. The drama ends when the victor maintains its display and the vanquished lowers its crest and sulks away in defeat—not as the result of any physical contact but simply from the comparative splendor of the "clothes" that the superior male has brought to this rather civilized contest. No blood flows. It is the hoofed version of a fashion show in which Valentino and Yves Saint Laurent have faced off on the runways of the African plains, an impressive display of civility in lieu of what might otherwise deteriorate into deadly confrontation.

Far away from the trading pits of Wall Street, lateral presentation offers irrefutable evidence that even among four-legged creatures, appearance counts . . . and often clothes do make the man.

Of Dangling Undies and Windsor Knots

Duvernois probably never heard the term _private equity_, but the lesson of his amusing story is just as relevant as ever. The sight of something terribly awry in the dress code of another is deflating in a business setting and often elicits a turn-off before a single word has been uttered. Thirty years ago, I went to a meeting in the hotel room of an entrepreneur who was seeking venture capital, only to discover a pair of his underwear hanging unceremoniously from one of the posts of his canopy bed. In my mind, the meeting was over before it ever began. I have absolutely no recollection of that gentleman's name, but I do have an indelible image of the scene imprinted in my mind and am quite certain that the offending undies were dangling from the lower left post as you faced the pillows from the bottom of the bed.

Thankfully, I have experienced other episodes at the opposite end of the apparel scale, where the impeccable attire of players in a business setting has immediately created a favorable impression—one of command and respect.

When I first joined the small venture capital firm that was my initiation into the industry, I felt sheepish at how out of place my bargain-basement threads looked compared with the partners' outfits of conservative suits, pastel-colored shirts with white cuffs and matching white collars, and silver tie bars that gave a distinctive lift to the Windsor knots at the top of their cravats. Within a few months, even though my meager savings had been depleted, Windsor knots on silk ties perfectly complemented my new pin-striped suits. When we entered a room together, the other side had trouble telling the difference between the full-fledged partners and the fledgling associate. Even when an exchange of business cards dispelled any lingering impression that I was a partner, I nevertheless felt like one and was ready to engage in battle. Like Tango on that street in Paris, I was distinguished in dress and brimming with freshly minted self-confidence.

Soon afterward, that card did read *Partner*—and eventually *Chairman of the Board*—but I never lost sight of Tango or of Duvernois's admonition that simple elegance in dress commands an initial flash of respect and, more importantly, an inner feeling that you are deserving of that burst of esteem. We need not resemble General Patton with a white steed, a riding crop, and knee-high leather boots—but a respectable imitation of Michael Douglas in the first version of *Wall Street* (prior to his arrest for securities fraud) is a good image to bear in mind.

If your grand entrance in a classic Bergdorf Goodman outfit is followed by your uttering a series of arrogant or bone-headed remarks, you might just as well head for the showers, for you have clearly squandered the advantage of making a good first impression. But if you seize the momentum with input as incisive as your outfit is elegant, the *book* and the *cover* of your presence will complement each other nicely and reinforce the initial impression that you are truly a force to be reckoned with.

Throwing the First Punch

Elegance in dress is a simple stratagem for success. It is neither an attempt to imitate the sharp-cheeked models with washboard abs that adorn the covers of *GQ*, nor is it an excuse for decorating oneself in the most avant-garde outfits from the runways of Paris or the fitting rooms of Milan. It is a gentle acknowledgment—for businessmen and businesswomen alike—that in the theater of commerce, we are often judged first by the wrapping and then by the contents. And therefore there is no reason *not* to get off on the right foot with an elegant wardrobe that exudes class and confidence—one that makes a statement that you are every bit as prepared to take command of the topic at hand as you are of your appearance. For men and women who walk onto the stage of business, *impressive* is just fine, but *jazzy* is not . . . and *smart* is a step forward, while *sexy* is for another time.

Clothes Make the Man

As our Parisian friend Tango learned while his colleagues were busy crossing over to the wrong side of the law, the most telling impact that classy attire will have is the one that becomes apparent when we look in the mirror. If we lift our chin a notch or two as a self-confident fellow stares back in the reflection, we just might lift our game a bit as well.

Donning the tasteful trappings of power is a simple, straightforward way to move in the direction of assuming power. We may think of it as the sartorial equivalent of a lion presenting itself with its impressive mane in full regalia. Clothes may not literally *make* the man, but clothes do reflect how a man or woman has chosen to present himself or herself to others. In the fisticuffs of brass-knuckle negotiations, substance may eventually win out over style—but style gets to throw the first punch.

Masters of Their Universe

Chapter Nine

The Clock Is Ticking

Masters of Their Universe

Secret #9

*Time is your most precious resource
and your most dreaded foe*

Masters of Their Universe

Dost thou love life? Then do not squander time,
for that's the stuff life is made of.

—Benjamin Franklin,
American statesman, scientist, and author

IN THE WORLD OF PRIVATE EQUITY, THE

most precious resource at our disposal is not money, but time—the limited number of hours that we have available to pour into the vessel of any pending project. Money is a commodity, but time is priceless. Far too often, participants in the realm of commerce waste prodigious amounts of time cramming their daily calendars from early rise to late collapse with a wave of conference calls and tedious meetings, even though only a few are reasonably calculated to advance a clearly articulated game plan.

MBA students hell-bent on a career in private equity might be well advised to take some time off from the rigors of study and the sterile lecture halls and head straight to the wilds of Africa for one week. At the Phinda Reserve in KwaZulu-Natal, South Africa, the four-day seminar in time management is taught by a handful of spotted fellows that roam the savannah grasslands by day and snooze at night. The syllabus for this seminar offers a heavy dose of good news: no finals, no lectures, no pop quizzes, and no dreaded cold calls in class by arrogant professors who relish the thought of dismembering your self-esteem.

The Cheetahs of Phinda: Master Timekeepers

Located just west of the Indian Ocean, the Phinda Reserve is renowned for the presence of cheetahs on its nearly 60,000 acres, and it rarely disappoints. I once tracked seven cheetahs there—a coalition of two males and a separate female with her four cubs—over a period of four straight days, from the crack of dawn until sunset each night. I never diverted my attention from those elegant creatures, content to photograph only the cheetahs and whatever else wandered into their field of play.

The cheetah is a daytime hunter and when the sun went down, so did those sleek cats, giving us human tagalongs a brief respite to return to camp, wolf down dinner, tend to our camera gear, hit the sack for a few hours, and then head back out the following day to link up with our spotted companions. We were usually able to track the adults in the early morning to a place not far from where we parted company the night before.

By following predators continuously over several days, you gain a great deal more insight into their behavior than is possible in the short snippets of time devoted to each species on a typical game drive. After a day or so with the cheetahs, I felt as if I had somehow insinuated myself into their midst and become a nonfeeding member of the clan. The rumble of our safari jeep had blended in with the rush of the wind, the incessant clicking of my shutter button no longer pricked up their ears, and the human scent of my presence had apparently been relegated in their consciousness to the same zone as the one occupied by a tree or a rock—neither predator nor prey and, thankfully, not edible.

It was a remarkable privilege to be accepted as part of the daily routine of those creatures. The time spent together allowed me to luxuriate in the sight of their magnificent physical assets. At rest, their hides appear to be stretched so tightly over muscles and sinews as not to allow a single ounce of fat to be found underneath; and at full tilt, their Lamborghini-like ability to accelerate from zero to 70 miles per hour in a few seconds has no equal.

But what stands out in my memory is how the cheetah manages the 99 percent of its day when it is not flying at the heels of an almost equally fleet-footed antelope. Relegated to one of the lowest rungs on the predator ladder—beneath stronger lions, leopards, and hyenas—the cheetah is barely able to survive in a habitat threatened by ever-widening human encroachment. And yet it endures, in great part due to its expert manipulation of time. It is a patient master in the art of hunting and a precise laser-guided missile of carnage when a target is within range.

Except in those instances in which males form coalitions, the adult cheetah is a solitary hunter. With only a limited supply of endurance, this feline predator must choose its quarry and its opportunities exceptionally well. If the actual chase persists for more than a few hundred yards, the cheetah's breathing rate and body temperature soar to the point where it must abort the hunt and allow itself to recover for up to half an hour before it may enter the fray again. And if its claws trip up a target in the few seconds before its reserves of energy are fully depleted, it must apply its chokehold silently and dine efficiently before a larger predator comes forward to claim the hard-earned fruits of its labor. Without the sheer brawn of the lion or the protection of a large clan, the cheetah must rely on its judicious use of time to survive—utilizing patience at one extreme and blinding speed at the other to carve out its niche in this precarious domain.

When Time Does Not Mean Money

We are all creatures of our past. Before launching my private equity career, I practiced law for six years as a corporate specialist. That period of apprenticeship was both the best training and the worst training for the investment career I was about to undertake. On the one hand, it prepared me to examine carefully the risk profile of any transaction, since it was my solemn duty as a lawyer to point out the soft underbelly of the deal to an unsuspecting client. This vigilance for uncovering the downside provided the yin to the wildcatting streak of yang that attracted me to the outsized rewards of private equity in the first place. On the other hand, lawyers charge by the hour, so being busy was confused in my mind with being productive.

By contrast, the investment business does not reward its athletes for the most time spent on the field. Instead, the profession rewards its players for time well spent. Solid bouts of strategic thinking about the merits of a prospective deal or deciphering when the trade winds favor exiting an investment may not consume much more time than the handful of hours it takes to roast a fourteen-pound turkey.

In the first year or two of my notably lackluster tenure as a young venture capitalist, I would delude myself into thinking that my long hours at the office—often unlocking the door before others arrived in the morning and flicking the lights off at night—were tantamount to a solid day in the trenches. It took me quite a while to adjust to the notion that in the investment world, unlike practicing law with a clock strapped to my ankle, a long day does not equate to a good day. It is often nothing more than just a very long day.

That painful lesson was learned more than thirty years ago at the expense of a series of high-technology deals that, in the parlance of the trade, "hit the wall" and left zeros on the scoreboard. Those portfolio losses came about in part because I failed to see the proverbial forest once I became lost in counting the leaves on individual trees. Buried in cash flow projections and obtuse financial statements, I never called a time-out to ask my more experienced colleagues, "Does anyone around here understand what this company does for a living, because I sure don't have the foggiest idea?" As a self-conscious novice in the field of venture capital, I had forgotten the most basic lesson: that there is no such thing as a dumb question if you don't know the answer. And taking a time-out to assess what we were doing wasn't in my nature yet—lawyers are not trained to take time-outs and stop the clock whose constant ticking means more billings.

The Uncivilized Wall Street Auction

As with the cheetahs of Phinda, one of the most critical decisions in the private equity field is figuring out which quarry are worth chasing and which will simply be a waste of precious time and energy. Unlike the one-on-one confrontation that pits a cheetah against its chosen prey, the standard technique for the sale of a portfolio company has evolved (some might say deteriorated) into an auction process. But in contrast with the highbrow auctions conducted by Sotheby's or Christie's, with numbered paddles and silver-tongued auctioneers, the private equity auction is not nearly as transparent. It is a much murkier affair in which a supposedly tight-lipped investment banker representing the seller sets all the rules and the tempo of the process and serves as the gateway for your access to information about the target company. Under the terms of a confidentiality agreement that all parties must sign, any contact with alternative bidders about their pricing expectations or strategies is strictly verboten. After a protracted process, the fate of the auction is determined by a final round of sealed bids.

Enticed to enter the bidding by flattery from the seller's investment banker that your firm has been handpicked as a very logical buyer, you are often assured that there will be only "a small handful" of other bidders and thus that your chances of emerging in the winner's circle are quite good. In the Pleistocene era of leveraged buyouts (just twenty or so years ago), a "handful" meant a handful, and you could safely assume that only about five (and certainly fewer than ten) competitors were on the field of battle. In the past two decades, however, the limbs of investment bankers have taken a detour on the road of evolution and today a "handful" may be measured more accurately by the leg extensions of a centipede.

With too many dollars chasing too few good deals, the typical Wall Street auction now proceeds through months of due diligence and multiple rounds of bidding in which a constantly shrinking number of suitors are urged to sharpen their pencils since "it is still too close to call." Eventually the auction process ends, and the "last man standing" wins— or loses for that matter, since the final price, by definition, exceeds what any other buyer on the face of the planet was willing to pay.

The Modified Cheetah Approach to Auctions

With only a few partners under the roof of our small buyout firm and thus a strong incentive not to waste time on frivolous chases, in more recent years we decided to forgo, whenever possible, the traditional auction process in favor of what might be referred to as the *modified cheetah approach*. More specifically, we often limited ourselves to one of two techniques for pursuing potential acquisitions: (1) a one-on-one negotiation between the "willing seller" and "willing buyer" (a throwback to the nearly extinct era of mid-twentieth-century deal making); or (2) a preemptive approach designed to cut short an auction and stop it dead in its tracks.

In the preemptive approach, we would enter the proceedings with the other contestants in the early phase of an auction, but warn the investment banker that we had no intention of lingering for more than a few weeks. At that point, we expected to either drop from the pack or immediately enter into exclusive negotiations at a sufficiently high price that the seller would be tempted to abandon the auction in favor of our more efficient preemptive approach and thus a shorter timetable to closing. Like the cheetah, we carefully selected very few targets and were usually true to our word of dropping from the auction festivities if our initial advances were ultimately rejected.

When Time Becomes Your Enemy

In the wild, once the cheetah manages to trip up its target, there is no victory dance or festive histrionics. At that critical juncture, the passage of time poses the greatest risk that the spoils of victory will quite literally be snatched from the jaws of the victor. Within a matter of minutes, a mob of vultures seems to materialize out of thin air, and there is the distinct risk that stronger land-based predators will close in and deprive the exhausted cheetah of its well-earned prize. Unlike the leopard, the cheetah does not have the strength to haul the carcass aloft into the security of a tree cache. It must feast in that narrow crevice between the exact moment of the kill and the time when the arrival of larger predators that had no hand in the capture may force it to leave the unfinished meal behind.

And so it is with the ticking of the clock after you have reached an agreement in principle with the seller to take its company off the market in exchange for your promise to pay a mutually acceptable price. At the moment the two sides shake hands on a yet-to-be-finalized agreement, they are standing on common ground—both buyer and seller want the deal to close. But until the day that money actually moves across the table, the deal is still at risk. At that point, it may be said that the passage of time works against closing the deal. A myriad of reasons can intervene to sidetrack the buyer or the seller from moving forward into the closing: severe gyrations in the capital markets may disrupt the buyer's financing commitments from other parties, regulatory authorities may interpose obstacles or extensive delays due to antitrust or other reasons, a competitor may announce a product breakthrough that disrupts the momentum of the deal, a key company executive may decide to resign in favor of greener pastures elsewhere, or a major customer or distributor may balk at the change of ownership.

In brief, the list of events that may disrupt the closing is virtually endless. Like the cheetah, both sides have their jaws clamped down on the throat of the deal, but external forces may pry those jaws apart. The ticking of the clock is no longer a welcome sound. Whether you are the buyer or the seller, the sweat on your brow is testament enough to the fact that the passage of time is the great enemy of closing any deal.

Of Sprints and Marathons

In the sport of track and field, it is rare indeed for any world-class athlete to compete in one of the sprints, which are over in just a few seconds, and the classic marathon, which unfolds over the span of more than two hours. The training, the muscle groups, the interplay of different body organs, and the psychology of the race are radically different from one event to the other. The sprint requires an all-out explosion and flurry of arms and legs pumping at blinding speed, while the marathon requires patience and savvy use of the limited resources of stamina and energy. But in both, the clock decides who wins and who loses.

In private equity, the financial athlete must be both the marathoner who carefully plots his course and patiently conserves his resources and the sprinter who erupts off the starting blocks at the prospect of capturing his chosen target, knowing that each tick of the clock before crossing the finish line is his greatest foe. In both phases of the deal business, time must be treated with tender loving care.

Masters of Their Universe

Chapter Ten

Fame

Masters of Their Universe

Secret #10

Day-old newspapers are used to wrap fish

Masters of Their Universe

What is fame? The advantage of being known
by people of whom you yourself know nothing,
and for whom you care as little.

—Lord Byron,
British poet and noted figure of the era of Romanticism

INSOFAR AS IT RELATES TO THE PURSUIT

of fame, the brief life of George Gordon Byron (1788–1824) is a prime example of the adage, "Do as I say, not as I do." Commonly known as Lord Byron, this writer and controversial figure was a study in contrasts. A prolific author of virtually limitless capacity (his works were ultimately published in a seventeen-volume compendium), Byron courted not only one amorous conquest after another but also the notoriety and fame that swirled around his flamboyant lifestyle.

Byron is widely considered to be the prototype of the modern-day celebrity, inspiring the moniker "Byronmania" (a label coined by his wife, Annabella) for the image and persona that so fascinated all of England. His penchant for serial affairs and dalliances found a place of literary immortality in his renowned magnum opus *Don Juan*. And his spirit of adventure and conquest lapped over into the military sphere, when Byron entered the fray on the rebel side of the Greek insurrection for independence from the Ottoman Empire—an improbable departure from his life of aristocratic excess that earned him a place of reverence in Greek history.

Hardly a model for the fiscal savvy required of private equity practitioners in more modern times, Byron's financial affairs were often upended by an abundance of personal debt and extravagance. But despite all the chaos in his life, Byron found peace and sanctuary in his extreme devotion to his beloved Newfoundland dog, Boatswain. Buried at Newstead Abbey in Nottinghamshire, Boatswain is honored with a monument larger than the one that marks Byron's grave, and the inscription in the poet's "Epitaph to a Dog" has immortalized this short-lived creature in one of Byron's most famous works. It reads in part:

> *Near this Spot are deposited the Remains of one*
> *who possessed Beauty without Vanity, Strength*
> *without Insolence, Courage without Ferocity, and*
> *all the Virtues of Man without his Vices. This praise,*
> *which would be unmeaning Flattery if inscribed over*
> *human Ashes, is but a just tribute to the Memory*
> *of BOATSWAIN, a DOG, who was born in*
> *Newfoundland May 1803, and died at Newstead*
> *Nov. 18th, 1808.*

A great lover of animals, Byron—both prolific and profligate in his personal life—found simplicity and virtue in the ways of the four-legged world. The absence of the madcap pursuit of fame by a creature such as Boatswain undoubtedly resonated with a figure who was both dismissive of and consumed by what others thought of his life and his work.

A Place Where Fame Has No Port of Entry

In the wild, there is no direct analogy to fame. Celebrity is a foreign notion altogether, postings on Facebook are nonexistent, and the endless streams of Twitter messages resonate not at all among creatures that seek out instead the life-sustaining streams of water populated with friend and foe alike. The only analogy to the newspaper articles that recount recent events are the droppings and scents left behind by creatures that have deposited their mark to be "read" closely by others. With their very pragmatic and unwavering focus on survival, both predator and prey are straightforward and goal-oriented in their routines, with very few detours along the way. Their route to survival is a path marked by forthright endeavor and unencumbered by flattery or deceit. I remember once commenting to a fellow photographer that one of the things I liked best about our safaris together in Botswana was the fact that the only traces of bullshit we ever ran into were the piles of dung left by African buffalos. Life in the savannah unfurls without interruption for standing ovations or curtain calls.

But not so within the labyrinthine canyons of Wall Street. In the world of high finance, image and notoriety count a great deal—not only in the eyes of your brethren in the trade but also when you stand alone in the morning and stare at the reflection in the mirror. The fame game is particularly rampant within the confines of Manhattan. I suppose that when you cram several million people inside a space not much larger than a few respectably sized Texas ranches, the rubbing of elbows among like-kind creatures eventually chafes at the skin, infecting the whole body with fever. The predators of Africa would never tolerate sharing such tight quarters with their competitors.

It is by no means an accident that image and profile are so crucial in the minds of many of the scions of another highly rewarded profession—the entertainment business. In that realm, a high profile that is constantly pushed in the face of the public is directly correlated with success. The most telling barometer of bankability in the entertainment world is not talent but exposure to the public's wide-eyed gaze. The Paris Hiltons and the Kim Kardashians of the world are testament enough that barrels of ink can be converted into a boatload of dollars through the alchemy of public fascination alone.

In the world of commerce, however, public exposure is not "standard equipment" on the vehicle that propels the business plan of an investment firm. It is nothing more than an option, much like fancy wire wheels: the vehicle will move just as well with less-exotic standard wheels, but the spoke version will be more noticeable to the gawkers on the side of the road. With very few exceptions, newspaper clippings that proclaim an investment firm's every move do nothing to advance the bottom line. In fact, with the public wrath that surged in the wake of the financial collapse of 2008, flak jackets and padded helmets became standard attire for the rainmakers of Wall Street, and the premium placed on obscurity never soared so high.

For the practitioners of private equity, focusing on the allure of public adulation is tantamount to taking your eye off the ball. As we move closer and closer to the glorious finale of a high-profile acquisition, all too often our hormones start raging through the body, stoking the ego with visions of the acclaim that awaits. With our ego aflame, we tend to let our guard down, and our due diligence antennae recede to half-mast as if to mourn the passing of our better judgment. Most of the senior partners at premier firms know this and accept it as a truism, but others are unable to resist the siren song of the High Temptress of Publicity. The buyout artist who surrenders to her seductive charms soon discovers that the pursuit of fame is the opium of the financial industry— it is mind-numbing, it is habit-forming, and it clouds your judgment in a fugue such that when you finally come to your senses, you are the last to realize that you have been operating in a dreamlike trance.

The Glare of the Bright Lights
Though certainly not the literary giant that Byron was, my beloved grandfather Arthur had a more pithy and pungent way of counseling against infatuation with fame in his constant admonition to "never forget that they use day-old newspaper to wrap fish." That precious bit of wisdom has served me well as a reminder that the approval of the public is a fleeting asset, while sound judgment has true endurance.

One of the many reasons I believe in the overarching role that providence plays in our destiny is the fact that, at one time or another, I have ignored virtually all the lessons taught by our four-legged professors and nevertheless lived to tell this tale as if I had religiously obeyed each of my own proscriptions.

The temptation to seek the klieg lights in my financial dealings is certainly no exception. More than twenty years ago, I gave in to that temptation and committed a grievous blunder—but was pardoned afterward by the hand of fate and given a chance to rehabilitate myself. That particular episode began one morning when I was downing my first cup of coffee and read an article in the business section about how a company at the fringes of the entertainment industry was under siege by a notorious corporate raider who had launched a hostile bid for control. On the surface (and all I did was barely scratch the surface in my research), the company had an enviable track record of growth and earnings. Normally reluctant to enter a high-profile contest for control of a public company, I thought that the freshly crowned barons of Dr Pepper should perhaps don the armor of a white knight and rescue this corporate damsel in distress. In the jargon of Wall Street, a white knight is a friendly suitor who attempts to dislodge the unsolicited grip of a hostile raider around the throat of an unwilling corporate target. The white knight offers the target a "kinder, gentler" form of being acquired in a transaction that its management finds to be more benign than the intentions of the nefarious corporate raider.

With all the highly publicized bravado of swashbuckling buyout artists, we swept in and rescued the takeover target from its plight, showering the shareholders whom we bought out with what (in retrospect) was an outrageously generous price. Within a matter of months, long after the headlines had faded, we suffered the rude awakening that our corporate damsel was a bit more sullied financially than we had any reason to suspect at the time of our hurried wedding. Revised cash flow projections proved to be nowhere near adequate to handle the humongous pile of debt that we had saddled the company with. We were soon headed for a day of reckoning we never thought possible when the newspaper headlines had sung our praises.

At least we recognized the titanic iceberg that lay ahead in time to change course, lending a receptive ear to another suitor intent on taking this company off our hands, apparently succumbing to its own desire to partake of the entertainment industry. Soon we had engineered an annulment of our marriage vows with the fair maiden, passing ownership on to the next in line, pocketing a tidy gain in the process, and side-stepping the loss that was imminent. We skulked back to our offices with no wounds to our pocketbooks but a much needed blow to our egos. Our nearly fatal flaw was a misplaced belief in our own Midas touch and a preoccupation with what others thought about our exploits.

The Lions of Tsavo

More than a century ago, a pair of maneless male lions found fame along the Tsavo River in Kenya, but it was not the kind of notoriety that befits this noble creature. For reasons still shrouded in mystery, the lions of Tsavo reputedly mauled and then devoured as many as 135 construction workers along the Kenya-Uganda Railway project during a nine-month reign of terror in 1898. With construction at a standstill, the head of the British project, Lt. Col. John Henry Patterson, pursued the Tsavo man-eaters and eventually shot and killed both, earning worldwide acclaim for his daring.

After stripping the hides from the lions and using them as rugs in his home for twenty-five years, Patterson sold the lion skins to Chicago's Field Museum to be stuffed and mounted as part of a permanent exhibit. Years ago, I attended a meeting at the Field Museum and was drawn to the display, only to be sadly disappointed with how unimpressive and slight in girth the famed Tsavo lions were, in part because the hides that wrapped the display figures had been trimmed down for their original use as trophy rugs.

I remember thinking at the time that the carcasses would have been better left alone at the spot where the lions were brought down, to be consumed by scavenging hyenas and thus recycled like everything else that lives and dies in the African plains. Fame is a distinctly human construct, and it had been thrust upon the lions of Tsavo in the aftermath of their grisly rampage. And perhaps like fame in the human world, for the two, it had come at too costly a price for my taste.

Be Careful What You Wish For

Though few of us aspire to be stuffed and mounted in a museum exhibit, to one degree or another, we all seek the admiration of our peers and others who are nameless and faceless but "out there" nevertheless. But the difference between being silently gratified that our exploits have found public favor and an obsession with fame is similar to the distinction between social drinking and alcoholism—one is a practice that does no harm, while the other is a disease that wreaks a path of havoc much wider than just the person with the glass in his hand.

It has often been said that success has many fathers, but that failure is an orphan. It could just as well be said that the blind courtship of fame produces only bastards.

The famous vaudeville comedian Fred Allen once commented, "A celebrity is a person who works hard all of their life to become well known, and then wears dark glasses to avoid being recognized." After years of photographing leopards in Africa—often called the ultimate stealth predator—it is apparent that the most skillful hunters know how to operate in hiding, acutely aware of the pitfalls of being noticed by others. To paraphrase Allen, those who aim to flourish in business would be well advised to work all of their lives in obscurity and save the dark glasses for a day at the beach.

Masters of Their Universe

Chapter
Eleven

When the Boat Comes Back

Masters of Their Universe

Secret #11

**The most underrated part of the
investment business is selling**

Masters of Their Universe

You get no thanks from your belly—it always forgets what
you've just done for it and comes begging again the next day.

—Aleksandr Solzhenitsyn,
Russian writer and activist

EVERY GREAT PERFORMANCE SHOULD BE
capped off by a memorable exit. Unlike Broadway plays,
in the investment business, success is measured not by the
number of consecutive nights your performance lingers on,
but rather by the difference between how well you buy and
how well you sell. Ownership itself is not the hallmark of
distinction but instead how astutely you learn to time and
engineer the passage of that ownership to another eager
practitioner of the trade. When we fall in love with one of
our companies—or with the accoutrements of ownership
such as the high profile that is often its companion—we
have lost sight of the fact that our job is *stewardship* (and
not parenthood) of our investment. Stewardship is only a
transitory job during which we manage the evolving maturity
of our protégé, whereas parenthood (as any parent knows so
well) is a permanent occupation.

Buying is a much ballyhooed but somewhat
exaggerated key to success in the investment business.
Winning an auction or other competitive process for buying
a company in one sense is the easiest thing in the world

to do—you simply have to pay more than what any other person on the face of the Earth is willing to pay for that asset. But knowing how and when to close out the show is a much more nuanced task that is rarely greeted with standing ovations from the investment world or the media.

I am reminded of a story told to me during the early days of my investment career. At the christening ceremonies for a brand-new ocean liner, a raucous crowd had gathered at the pier near the bow of the pristine cruiser. Bands were playing, confetti rained down from the rails of the ship, and champagne flowed as the vessel was loosened from its moorings and slipped out to sea for its maiden voyage. Everyone in the crowd was swept up in the frenzy of the moment—all except a little old man with a bushy mustache wearing a trench coat and Homburg, who just leaned forward on his cane and watched the scene unfold through the small round spectacles perched on his nose. At last, exasperated by the reserved demeanor of the little old man, one of the fresh-faced revelers confronted him and blurted out, "Everyone else is cheering and drinking and tossing confetti in the air, and you just stand there like a bump on a log. What's the matter with you, old man?" The elderly gentleman turned to his young inquisitor, adjusted his spectacles, and replied matter-of-factly, "I'll cheer when the boat comes back."

When the Closing Is an Opening

In the investment business, there are too few little old men wearing simple trench coats and Homburgs and far too many revelers at the launch of our ocean liners. All the hoopla is reserved for acquisitions, while the stillness that often surrounds the art of selling is deafening. It is counterintuitive to be so festive at the front end of the investment process and so serene at the back end—at the time of purchase, you take the money *out* of your pocket and hand it to someone else, while at the time of sale, hopefully you stuff your pockets to the brim with the fruits of your labor.

Over the years, I've been invited to dozens of "closing parties" to celebrate the purchase of a company, but hardly any to celebrate the sale. The term *closing* is even somewhat of a misnomer—for the buyer, it should be called an *opening*, and the term *closing* should be reserved as the exclusive province of the seller, who is, after all, closing out a chapter in the chronicle of its portfolio. Even the headlines of *The Wall Street Journal* usually declare "Jones Purchases Acme Corporation" and not "Smith Sells Control of Acme." And within the industry itself, the respective emotions of exultation and hushed restraint seem to mirror the headlines—buyers revel at a pitch that drowns out the soft murmurings of the sellers.

The Quiet Triumph of the Hunter

The creatures in the African bush seem to have arranged things differently. The hunt itself is a very restrained, methodical, dead-serious affair. The sight of prey animals such as zebra or buffalo entering the zone of potential capture triggers immediate silence and stealth within a band of hunting lions. There is a palpable tensing of the muscles, a pricking of the ears, crouching down in the tall grass, and intense surveying of the field of play to plot their strategy. Any sounds at all in the vicinity are viewed as a diversion and a possible alarm that may spook the herd. It is only after the hunt is over and the prey brought down that there is the slightest echo of celebration. Lions may bellow a roar of dominion over the fallen prey, and wild dogs wag their tails furiously (but silently) while wolfing down the prize of a successful hunt. The predators of Africa know full well that letting your guard down has no place in the African bush, at least not until after all the work is done and the fruits of the deal are digested.

A Carbonated Tour de Force

Rarely does a single episode of negotiations provide the opportunity to bring to bear each of the secrets taught by our four-legged professors. But the sale of our interests in the Dr Pepper/7-Up Companies was no ordinary deal—it was the pinnacle of our investment firm's track record up to that time, and a high-wire act that unfolded in a three-ringed circus of Wall Street haggling. Our firm's role was not only to serve as the master of ceremonies in coordinating the multiple sets of negotiations, but also as the lion-tamer that kept the financial predators away from each other's throats.

To set the stage with the _dramatis personae_ in this true-life adventure, our Dallas investment firm Hicks & Haas (H&H) led the acquisition of Dr Pepper Company in August 1986 with financial backing from Lehman Brothers and consumer giant Cadbury-Schweppes. Just a few months later, after both Lehman and Cadbury declined to finance our efforts to buy The 7-Up Company from cigarette kingpin Philip Morris, H&H scrambled to secure the needed financing for the 7-Up buyout from Wall Street potentates Donaldson Lufkin Jenrette (DLJ) and Citicorp

Venture Capital. Forced by the unwillingness of Lehman and Cadbury to participate in the 7-Up deal, we separated Dr Pepper and 7-Up into two different ownership structures and cobbled together an agreement between the two that allowed a single team of senior managers to direct the operations of both companies without running afoul of the antitrust rules that might otherwise prohibit such conduct.

And we were off to the races. In the year after the acquisitions, Dr Pepper continued to rack up impressive growth in earnings while 7-Up engineered a dramatic turnaround from the humdrum performance of its years as a neglected stepchild of Philip Morris. By the end of 1987 (our first full year of ownership), Dr Pepper and 7-Up had compiled a torrid pace of combined growth, earning a total of $111 million in operating profits compared to just $58 million in the prior year.

Before our bubble had a chance to burst, we placed a figurative For Sale sign on the front lawn of the headquarters of our soft drink group and welcomed all bidders to come forth with their best offers. In the privacy of our own inner sanctum, we were hoping for a total price of around $1 billion for the two pieces of merchandise combined, which would have netted a tidy profit of close to $350 million to be split among our firm and its co-investors in Dr Pepper and 7-Up in the span of only about eighteen months of ownership. At a price of $1 billion, it would have been a "tape-measure home run" in the jargon of Wall Street.

But rather than wait for bids to come over the transom through our investment bankers, H&H decided to reach out to a close friend and colleague who had just launched a new private equity fund with backing from

Prudential Insurance. Unencumbered by the Gordian knots that often entangle such complex transactions, we met privately on several occasions—in such nondescript settings as an all-night hamburger joint in midtown Manhattan—in an effort to hash out a bargain that worked for both sides. And lo and behold, we did just that in a fraction of the time that our investment bankers had slated for the sale process.

What emerged from those private negotiations was an eye-popping deal for the shareholders of Dr Pepper and 7-Up—we were to receive $1.3 billion for our collective investments (a gain of almost $650 million compared to the $350 million we had targeted), and furthermore we would be able to leave a portion of our gain invested in the two companies in exchange for continuing to hold a controlling interest in the newly named and unified Dr Pepper/7-Up Companies.

To avoid a Byzantine labyrinth of state insurance regulations, Prudential was required to own less than 50 percent of the combined enterprise, so it needed a knowledgeable and trustworthy partner that would be willing to invest capital for a 51 percent ownership stake. H&H and our investment cohorts in the Dr Pepper and 7-Up deals filled the bill just fine as a ready and willing set of partners, and thus we had the chance to realize a huge gain, maintain controlling interest, and saddle up for another ride.

Let the Lion-Taming Begin

In addition to the usual complexities of papering the deal (a patchwork quilt of merger and financing agreements), there was one other highly unusual obstacle that lay ahead.

The deal with Prudential had come together with such warp speed that we had not yet had a chance to pound out an agreement between the major institutional shareholders of Dr Pepper (Lehman and Cadbury) and their counterparts on the 7-Up side (DLJ and Citicorp) as to how we would split the proceeds of sale in the event of a single deal for both companies rather than two separate deals.

Since our firm H&H owned almost exactly the same percentage interest in each company, we were indifferent to the split and therefore in a unique position to act as an "honest broker" in the ensuing negotiations as to how we would carve up the overstuffed turkey that had arrived on our doorstep well before the scheduled date for Thanksgiving.

There is only one scene on Wall Street more gruesome than witnessing a band of institutions hurling blame on each other for a deal that has gone sour—and that is being in the midst of the feeding frenzy that ensues when financial giants are called upon to decide how to divvy up an unexpectedly large gain.

With the Prudential offer hanging in the balance as both a dangling carrot that should have promoted cooperation among the parties and a piñata to be pounded by the club carriers of Wall Street, the action shifted to the sellers' side of the table and our efforts to stitch together a deal between the Dr Pepper and 7-Up shareholders on the overall split of the proceeds. This fraternal rivalry pitted Lehman and Cadbury on the Dr Pepper side versus DLJ and Citicorp on the 7-Up side, with our firm squarely in the middle wearing the black-and-white stripes of the impartial referee.

It soon became apparent that we might just as well have been wearing the black-and-white stripes of a zebra in the midst of a clan of frenzied hyenas. A short series of conference calls among the parties left little doubt that we were not headed anywhere near consensus, so we all thought it best for our firm to assume the role of shuttle diplomat à la Henry Kissinger. With Kissinger as our role model, we implemented each of the secrets in our dog-eared manual on the art of negotiation.

Secret #6: *Know the limits of your own territory—perhaps the world is flat after all*

The first decision was designating the site for our face-to-face negotiations, and we chose Dallas, inviting each of the parties to our offices as neutral turf that favored neither the Dr Pepper nor the 7-Up side. In addition to extracting the opposing parties from the tension and peer pressure that ooze out of the sidewalks of New York, the Texas site put H&H on our home territory. In the more hospitable atmosphere that pervades Dallas, we felt we could exert greater control over the ensuing discussions than if we were gridlocked in the snarling pace of Gotham. In our role as deal maker, we would benefit from all the intangibles of home-field advantage whereas in New York we would be relegated to the visitors' dugout.

Besides the comfort of being on our home turf, staging the negotiations in Dallas reinforced the impression that the US soft drink sector was one where our firm was more steeped in experience than any of the other financial participants. As the site of the headquarters for both Dr Pepper and 7-Up (as well as the Dr Pepper Bottling Group of Texas, another of our holdings), we would be meeting at the epicenter of a cluster of our portfolio companies that represented the third largest soft drink group in the country. In the intense negotiations that were about to unfold, we had set ourselves up as the gracious hosts, but also as the firm that was most familiar with the territory we were about to explore in search of common ground.

Secret #8: <u>*Don't kid yourself—appearance counts*</u>

Once all parties converged on the Republic of Texas, we ushered everyone into our offices on the penthouse floor of the most exclusive office complex in Dallas—an elegant setting outfitted with Regency-era furniture, eighteenth- and nineteenth-century antiques, oriental rugs, and a conference room with a semicircular window that stretched almost the length of a squash court. The only thing that might not have been genuine was the impression that we could afford the furnishings at the time we decorated our offices.

Admittedly, there was a madness to our method, but there was also a method to our madness. By decorating our offices to the hilt, we were banking on the theory that an office that exudes Tiffany quality also exudes success. In the back of our minds, we might also have figured that if our fledgling firm were destined to crash and burn, the story of our demise would be covered by both a squib in *The Wall Street Journal* and a feature layout in *Architectural Digest*.

When colleagues first visited our offices, there was often a visible sagging of the shoulders and a slight drop of the jaw. Everyone noticed—and no one failed to comment on—the décor. We would respond with the obligatory "aw shucks" and a wisecrack that we had "furnished it one deal at a time" (more truth than fiction), but it never failed to impress and to tilt the home-field advantage just a tad more in our favor.

Secret #5: *Your eyes are the most potent weapon in your arsenal*

Once all the players were assembled on stage, it was time to loosen our ties, roll up our sleeves, and get down to the business of divvying up the spoils of the Prudential deal. On the Dr Pepper side of the table, Lehman took the lead in advancing the cause of the Pepper shareholders, while DLJ did the same on behalf of the 7-Up stakeholders.

With Lehman and DLJ free to face off at will with only occasional intervention from our firm, the first day produced nothing but rigid positions, harsh rhetoric, and a stack of boxes of partially consumed pizza that we had ordered in for dinner. Like two knights jousting on horseback, the Lehman and DLJ bankers bashed their lances against each other all day long, with no visible signs of progress. But unlike armored knights, in this jousting session, their visors were raised and their eyes visible. As the day wore on, the amount of tension and frustration that had overtaken the conference room was visible in the glares they exchanged as well as in their verbal barbs. Brilliant colleagues who genuinely respected each other were working themselves into a frenzy, egged on by periodic input from the powers-that-be at their respective firms back in New York. The negotiations were in danger of spinning out of control when we adjourned for the day, exhausted and discouraged. Downcast eyes told it all—we were on the verge of blowing the chance to collect an ungodly jackpot, all because of intramural warfare.

Secret #4: *In the long run, integrity trumps the fleeting advantages of artifice*

Secret #7: *In a negotiation, you have as much leverage as the other side thinks you have*

Clearly, a different strategy was called for on the second day lest we deteriorate from stale pizza to a complete breakdown. So we enforced a new ground rule: the Lehman representatives would be confined to one conference room and the DLJ emissaries to a separate one, and the partners from our firm would shuttle back and forth in an effort to stitch together a deal. Relieved of the pressure to be the ultimate bad boy in the room, the separated principals visibly relaxed. And the H&H diplomats wore a groove in our oriental rugs traipsing back and forth between the Dr Pepper command center and the 7-Up bailiwick.

There was a strange dynamic at work that day. Two heavily muscled New York investment firms that were used to fighting their own battles (and who controlled far more of the stock of Dr Pepper and 7-Up than did H&H) allowed themselves to be disengaged from the direct dueling that is one of the hallmarks of Wall Street lore. If either one had shouted out heavyweight champion John L. Sullivan's immortal line "I can lick any son of a bitch in the house," it would have fallen on deaf ears, since their adversaries were safely out of range in another conference room.

Buoyed by a crest of credibility from the success of our one-on-one deal making with Prudential and insulated from any charges of favoritism by virtue of our firm's equal stake in the two concerns, H&H could don the mantle of impartiality. Our firm certainly didn't have the clout to impose any particular settlement, but we did have the *perceived* leverage that in the eyes of the two opposing factions we had become indispensable to forging an agreement and could clearly be trusted to play it straight. Even in the absence of any overriding power, our small firm wielded a great deal of influence over the ensuing negotiations, simply because we could dialogue calmly and knowledgeably with both parties, all the while enjoying their unqualified trust.

Secret #1: *When in doubt, make the more correctable mistake*

Secret #2: *Life is a contact sport, so stay focused on the end zone*

Eventually, it became apparent that we were making headway in bridging a chasm that only one day earlier had seemed uncrossable. But often in negotiations, the last 5 percent of the gap between opposing parties is the most difficult to close. Each side is convinced to a moral certainty that it has gone more than halfway already and thus *deserves* that last 5 percent. Staking out self-declared final positions, the parties draw more lines in the sand than a group of five-year-olds at a birthday party on the beach. By that point, righteous indignation has settled in, the coffee has baked to the consistency of motor oil, and patience has worn threadbare. And this deal was no exception.

Once we reconvened as a single group in the large conference room to pound out a compromise on the remaining gap between their respective positions, each side swore that it was at its "choke point," and the Lehman delegates threatened to catch the next flight out of Dallas unless DLJ buckled to its final demands. We had come a long way, but the issue was now being framed by the opposing factions in macho terms as if their manhood were at stake rather than the last 5 percentage points of a deal that was already 30 percent richer than we had ever expected it to be. Like naughty children, it was time for the kids to be banished once again to their separate conference rooms.

The "fly in the ointment" of attempting to reach final agreement was the fact that 7-Up had posted a huge jump in operating profits in 1987, but it was only the first solid year in its recent history, whereas Dr Pepper had been consistently profitable year after year but not quite as impressive as 7-Up over the past twelve months. In a teeter-totter version of shuttle diplomacy, on this very point H&H would privately attempt to turn each side's argument on its head to nudge the parties toward consensus. On the Pepper side, Lehman argued that 7-Up's spectacular year might just have been a "flash in the pan" and did not deserve to be valued as richly as Dr Pepper's unbroken string of highly profitable years— to which we would respond by pointing out that if 7-Up's growth trajectory were to continue for even one more year, the Pepper shareholders would end up with a much worse split in any future negotiations. In the opposing conference room, citing the same numbers, DLJ would dig in its heels on the basis that 7-Up's sensational growth deserved to be valued *more* highly since it represented a disproportionate share of the combined jump in earnings in 1987—and we would respond by cautioning that the past year might just have been a "flash in the pan" (plagiarizing our Lehman friends in the other room). No one was right and no one was wrong . . . but no one was prepared to concede anything just yet.

The scene reminded me of the faux skirmishes that feasting lions will sometimes stage after working together to bring down an eight-hundred-pound Grevy's zebra. Jockeying for position along the sides of the freshly fallen carcass, the lions at first will snarl and swipe at each other, but no one leaves the dinner table—those big cats are all bright enough to know that their time is better spent just munching away on a meal that is more than adequate to satisfy everyone's hunger, rather than sparring over the spoils of a hugely successful hunt.

Convinced of the futility of attempting to budge either side from the *righteousness* of its position, H&H leaned into our colleagues with a heavy dose of realpolitik, repeatedly urging each side to concentrate on the so-called end zone: "You have no choice but to compromise here— you're not going to walk away from a $1.3 billion payday, are you?" . . . "Stop focusing on what's on the other side's plate and focus on what's on yours—that's a big enough meal for you, don't you think?" . . . "You're so far into the gravy zone here that you're forgetting why you saddled up on this investment in the first place."

After a while, it began to settle in with both sides that neither one was about to cave in to the other's demands and that we should abandon the shadowy merits of the arguments in favor of the fact that we had no option left but to compromise. A few trial balloons were floated from one conference room to the other, and with a bit of prodding and cajoling, the focus turned to the exact contours of the settlement. I remember our offering up a few reminders that we must avoid making the uncorrectable mistake:

"Stop threatening to walk out of here and head back to New York—no one in their right mind is going to leave this deal dangling in the wind!" . . . "You know we're going to split the difference somehow, so let's all calm down and find that middle ground." . . . "Once we close the gap here, you'll return home to the Wall Street equivalent of a ticker tape parade—and one year from now, you'll have trouble remembering how we split the last few percent."

Eventually, the prospect of *not* reaching consensus became untenable. At this sensitive stage in the negotiations, what we did was to sharpen Lehman's and DLJ's focus on the end zone and the fact that walking away in a huff would have been a dreadfully uncorrectable mistake.

Secret #3: *Know your weaknesses as well as you know your strengths*

In retrospect, there wasn't anything particularly brilliant about our firm's shuttle diplomacy. Nothing brilliant at all—just the same thing any respectable clan of predators would have done in similar circumstances. After all, we were just a bunch of hungry lions eyeing the plump zebra that had fallen in our laps.

But it was a task demanding of the skills of two different lion-tamers if the negotiations were eventually to reach closure. The Lehman and DLJ protagonists on either side of the deal normally lorded over their own turf in the canyons of Wall Street, and even our spacious offices in Dallas were a tad too snug for long-term cohabitation among predators. For H&H to prevail in our efforts to lead the parties to common ground, we needed to blend together the scalloped edges of personal diplomacy with the callous reality of hard-nosed negotiating. Those two skills—adroit diplomacy and sharp-elbowed bargaining—are rarely housed in equal measure inside the confines of the same body. We fully realized that when Messrs. Hicks and Haas formed Hicks & Haas and brought together under one roof the divergent talents and personalities of its two founders. The periodic separation of the two negotiating factions into different conference rooms allowed one H&H partner to smooth ruffled feathers while the other twisted arms just a few feet away, all in pursuit of the same goal.

Secret #9: *Time is your most precious resource and your most dreaded foe*

Perseverance and a bit of creativity eventually carried the day as we used Elmer's glue to attach one final Lehman proposal to the mosaic of compromise and a handful of baling wire to wrap in one of DLJ's last demands. It definitely wasn't a piece of art, but it was deal making.

At long last, there was consensus on a somewhat convoluted but mutually acceptable sharing arrangement: out of the total profits from the deal, the Dr Pepper side would receive the first $60 million of gain, the two sides would share evenly in the next $550 million, and any profits above that would be split 57.5 percent to the Dr Pepper side and 42.5 percent to the 7-Up side. We had a handshake among the negotiators in Dallas, but we all knew that the tentative agreement might well dissolve the minute each of the two sets of investors set foot back in their respective offices in Manhattan and second-guessing colleagues swooped in like vultures to pick away at the terms of the deal. The passage of time would serve only to undermine our fragile consensus if we waited even a few days to have it ratified by their Manhattan cohorts.

We were all united in our desire to bring the marathon negotiations to a close and not allow the ticking of the clock to work against our arrangement. Capitalizing on the momentum of the moment, the representatives of Lehman and DLJ wasted no time in calling their respective offices in New York and securing final approval. Arms reached across the table, hands clasped, and we walked away secure in the knowledge that this deal was destined to head toward a closing.

Secret #10: *Day-old newspapers are used to wrap fish*

There was little doubt in our minds at the time of the Dr Pepper/7-Up negotiations that we were in the midst of a transaction that would become one of the storied episodes in LBO history. In the span of less than two years, we had assembled a soft drink juggernaut, avoided the crushing footsteps of the two gorillas in the jungle (Coke and Pepsi), and arranged both a lucrative exit and an encore performance with another round of upside potential. Everyone who had a part in the script genuinely believed that this deal would be heralded for years to come.

In retrospect, there was only one thing that kept my feet planted firmly on the ground: a desire to realize the ambitions that had driven me into the investment business in the first place. It was exactly the same centripetal force that keeps a clan of predators focused on a common target whenever cooperative action is called for. During the negotiations with Prudential and later with the Dr Pepper/7-Up stakeholders, our firm had only one objective in mind—harvesting what we perceived to be the fruits of a hard-earned victory. And not just any victory—this was the mother lode. In my mind, it was never about impressing the titans of Wall Street or pinning bragging rights on my lapels for the next black-tie affair in the theater district.

The newspaper articles and industry scuttlebutt that would trumpet our achievements were flattering to be sure, and yet newsprint rubs off on your hands, the articles yellow with time, and the sound of the ovations soon fades away. But when you are in a position to don a bullet-proof vest and avoid the future missteps that would strip you of that priceless garment, you have reached the destination of your chosen journey. And when your ship pulls into port, there may not be throngs of people awaiting your return, perhaps just a little old man in a frumpy trench coat and Homburg standing all by himself applauding as you fasten your moorings to the dock. After all, he did promise to cheer when the boat came back.

Epilogue

The View from My Angle

Masters of Their Universe

Secret #12

*There are only two things that
are a matter of life and death:
life and death*

Masters of Their Universe

It's not that I'm afraid to die.
I just don't want to be there when it happens.

—Woody Allen,
American film writer, director, and actor

AT THE END OF A LONG JOURNEY, WE TEND

to look back on the miles crossed and see things differently than we did when we were in the midst of the journey. Everything looks different in hindsight. It's something we call *perspective.* An $11-per-week boarding house that became my abode in high school no longer seems so dusty and dreary, but rather as a place to start fresh and savor everything accumulated after that. Heart arrhythmias no longer feel like near-death experiences, but rather as catalysts for appreciating the privilege of being able to grow old gracefully. Even dreadful venture capital deals feel like the tuition paid to enter the halls of higher learning at Leveraged Buyout University.

Perhaps the secret to gaining perspective as we journey along the way—and not waiting for life's odyssey to be almost at an end—is realizing that the words *crisis* and *calamity* and *disaster* must be judiciously reserved for only a few life events, and that only *life* and *death* are indeed matters of life and death.

Life Along the Razor's Edge

More so than any other place on earth, Africa tends to cast a spell over those who partake of the exotic beings that prowl its savannah grasslands and wander across its forbidding deserts. It is there that we sample a world radically different from our own and walk away forever changed, sensing that we have been privileged to cross over into a realm that surpasses our own not only in its imposing grandeur but also in the raw, yet refined, wisdom of its inhabitants.

Perhaps it is because we chuck the gadgets of modernity in a place that is timeless. Perhaps because we witness life and death along the razor's edge that separates the two. Perhaps because we marvel at the resilience of creatures that suffer loss and never miss a beat returning to the fray—cheetah mothers whose cubs succumb to the perils of the plains while she trundles on with the ones that still remain, and lionesses that promptly enter a state of estrus to usher in a fresh batch of the young after watching a newly crowned head of pride maul her cubs as the unwelcome reminder of its predecessor.

What is unclear is the extent to which those animals experience *suffering*—physical as well as emotional—the way we do or whether that is a construct we import from our world and overlay on theirs. What is undeniable, however, is that both predator and prey spend virtually every day poised on the edge between survival and death, and yet somehow manage to display uncanny equanimity amongst all that risk.

When we observe the denizens of the wild with nothing more powerful than a simple point-and-shoot camera, we see creatures at their very best—daring in the extreme, focused on the survival of their young, incapable of killing for sport or revenge, and undistracted by rigid notions of right and wrong. And when we return home to care for our own canine clans, we see *ourselves* at our very best: unselfish, devoted, honest, and compassionate. It should come as no great surprise then that both venues serve as fertile ground for the growing and harvesting of life lessons.

Losing It All

The secrets taught by four-legged professors are much like the gadgets that make up a thief's set of lock picks. Inside the zippered pouch of a sophisticated burglar, there is an ingenious array of odd-shaped tools that may be used to pry open almost any door regardless of its vintage or locking mechanism. And so it is with the teachings of four-legged professors, both those that roam free and must hunt to survive as well as the ones who eat from ceramic bowls and sleep on stuffed pillows at night. Their teachings offer up the tools to open many of the doors we must each pass through, whether in business or elsewhere in the labyrinth of our lives.

Creatures in the wild have left distinct clues about life lessons that extend far beyond the borders of their universe. *Gluttony*—How fat animals are more easily taken down than the ones that remain trim and in battle-ready condition. *Obsession*—How the pursuit of the material beyond the point where it enhances your life and that of clan mates who depend on you may be a useless expenditure of energy. *Risk*—How the world is a precarious place where you never quite find a safe haven from the forces of disease and loss that may reverse the success of prior hunts.

Despite all the good fortune that has come my way in

business—or perhaps because of the magnitude and rapidity with which it arrived on my doorstep—I have always been suspicious of its permanence. While this fear has dissipated over time, I have never completely lost the sense of dread that the black holes of gluttony, obsession, and risk could somehow conspire to knock on my door at any moment and announce that the package of prosperity had been delivered to the wrong address. Although it is often given a bad rap, paranoia can become your best ally in such circumstances, for it is the antidote to the hubris that has brought down many a castle once thought to be impregnable.

This fear of "losing it all in a heartbeat" dovetails with my belief that many who succeed in business do so more out of a fear of failure than a thirst for success . . . and many who end up failing do so out of a misplaced infatuation with success. For anyone who has ever rumbled around the African plains in a jeep, it is evident that a healthy dose of paranoia—flinching at unfamiliar sounds, scampering up trees at the mere sight of a rival on the prowl, breaking out in a stampede when a herd-mate catches the slightest whiff of danger—often separates the survivors from whatever may be featured on the menu du jour.

A Graceful Exit

I have always thought that I tend to absorb life lessons best when I am either most content or least content and therefore highly receptive to whatever has induced the peaks and valleys of my emotions. I was never more content than when I captured images of those four-legged magicians in Africa or when I strolled beside my clan of mutts and marveled at their very basic approach to life, as if they had apprenticed with Thoreau at Walden Pond. In both settings, I became infatuated with the *simplicity* of it all, the near total absence of distractions and the sense that I had somehow managed to shed for the moment the complications of a very complicated life.

Within the African wilderness and at peace among my clan of mixed breeds, the sometimes tedious pursuit of money was relevant only in the sense that its attainment afforded leave to follow other paths that were a welcome diversion from the well-trodden thoroughfares of business. With my guard down and my mind free to wander, I was well prepared to absorb as many of the lessons as were revealed in such halcyon times.

At the opposite end of the spectrum, some of my most distressing moments have unveiled secrets of a very different sort. While the players on the African stage perform every day and night in a life-and-death drama, it was two of the guys in our own canine clan who bestowed a priceless set of lessons about the life arc that all of us are on.

I watched in awe as Oliver, the most senior member of the clan, waged a gallant battle against the maladies of blindness, deafness, paralysis, and lung disease to live another three years beyond the "few more days" that medical experts had predicted—and in the process, I attended his daily tutorial on the art of handling adversity and adjusting to the "thousand natural shocks" that his flesh had been heir to.

Meanwhile, Oliver's fourteen-year-old brother Elmer managed to live with dignity one day at a time in the final stages of his bout with liver cancer—and in Elmer's classroom, I learned how to lose a loved one through the alchemy of spinning lasting memories out of fleeting moments.

Much like an accomplished wildlife photographer, Oliver and Elmer adjusted their sights to unforeseen circumstances in order to capture the essence of what presented itself in the viewfinder. The tribulations of these two senior citizens—one content to move about in the canine equivalent of a wheelchair and the other able to face his final days with grace—have also served as a primer for coming to grips with the inevitability of my own decline. As the poet Sylvia Plath reminds us, "Dying is an art, like everything else."

Though not taught at business school, Oliver's and Elmer's courses offer a poignant perspective on the *limitations* inherent in our pursuit of fortune—how the seemingly overwhelming importance of a merger negotiation dissolves in an instant when the results of a biopsy are revealed, and how a 50 percent leap in earnings for one of our portfolio companies is only a baby step compared with Oliver's ability to trundle along in his wheelchair after months of therapy. In the courses offered by these two professors, I learned to define *crisis* and *triumph* and *nobility* a bit differently than may be taught in business school. Money has a seat in the back of their classrooms (a "back bencher" in the parlance of graduate school) for the simple reason that it affords the wherewithal to spare no expense in seeking out the very best veterinarians, therapists, and treatment options. In the midst of a health crisis, money is the currency that sometimes affords you the chance to extend the life of a creature you love and who loves you back. And at the end of the day, you cast an appreciative glance toward that back bencher, for it has performed its chosen task extremely well.

The escapes to Africa taught me how to experience

timelessness, while Oliver's tenacity and Elmer's ordeals taught me how to measure time in days or even hours. And it was at such moments—when I felt the exquisite sorcery of Africa and the equally exquisite pain of impending loss— that I gained the greatest sense of appreciation for the lessons taught by four-legged professors.

A Final Nod to Good Fortune

The German poet and philosopher Johann Friedrich von Schiller once commented that "one can advise comfortably from a safe port." And indeed, one of the privileges of having attained a certain measure of success in business is the fact that, whether deserved or not, your advice is afforded considerably greater weight than the counsel of someone who failed to triumph on the battlefield of commerce or another who never entered the fray at all.

Though often cast in the role of an advisor in my lectures and writings, I am still grounded by the deep-seated belief that sheer providence deserves the lion's share of the credit for my good fortune. Five hundred years ago, Niccolò Machiavelli urged in his seminal work *The Prince* that we all tip our hat to the vagaries of chance whenever we are tempted to take undue ownership of our successes: "I hold it to be true that Fortune is the arbiter of one-half of our actions, but that she still leaves us to direct the other half, or perhaps a little less." If half the credit still be mine, I will share that half with the four-legged creatures whose uncommon dignity, mettle, and wisdom have left indelible paw prints in my mind and whose peerless secrets have been whispered in my ear in a language that we would all do well to listen to.

Masters of Their Universe